Period Tracker

JOURNAL & DIARY

THIS BOOK BELONGS TO

_____

How To Use This Book

1 | The circles at the top of each monthly spread correspond to the month. Fill in accordingly.

2 | Using the key, shade a square daily once your period begins. You can use gel pens, colored pencils, highlighters, or stickers.

3 | Each day, check mark any symptoms and rate other symptoms using the smiley face scale.

4 | There is space each day to jot down a few notes or journal feelings, additional symptoms, or medications.

5 | Count the number of days since your day 1 of the prior month. That is your cycle length!

6 | Predict when to expect your next period based upon your cycle length. This will help you to determine if your cycles are regular.

8 | There are 48 monthly spreads in this journal giving you space to track your period for two years.

♥

| J | F | M | A | M | J | J | A | S | O | N | D |

1	2	3	4	5	6	7	8	9	10	11	12
13	14	15	16	17	18	19	20	21	22	23	24
25	26	27	28	29	30	31					

*Cross off dates that do not apply this month

KEY: ■ HEAVY ◪ MEDIUM ◫ LIGHT • SPOTTING ⊠ N/A

_____ DAYS SINCE LAST PERIOD ♥ EXPECT NEXT PERIOD AROUND _____

Day 1 of Cycle

CRAVINGS ☐   BACKACHE ☐   ENERGY ☺ ☺ ☹
ACNE ☐   HEADACHE ☐   MOOD ☺ ☺ ☹
CRAMPS ☐   SORE BREASTS ☐   SLEEP ☺ ☺ ☹

....
....
....

Day 2 of Cycle

CRAVINGS ☐   BACKACHE ☐   ENERGY ☺ ☺ ☹
ACNE ☐   HEADACHE ☐   MOOD ☺ ☺ ☹
CRAMPS ☐   SORE BREASTS ☐   SLEEP ☺ ☺ ☹

....
....
....

Day 3 of Cycle

CRAVINGS ☐   BACKACHE ☐   ENERGY ☺ ☺ ☹
ACNE ☐   HEADACHE ☐   MOOD ☺ ☺ ☹
CRAMPS ☐   SORE BREASTS ☐   SLEEP ☺ ☺ ☹

....
....
....

Day 4 of Cycle

CRAVINGS ☐   BACKACHE ☐   ENERGY 😊 😐 ☹️
ACNE ☐   HEADACHE ☐   MOOD 😊 😐 ☹️
CRAMPS ☐   SORE BREASTS ☐   SLEEP 😊 😐 ☹️

....
....
....

Day 5 of Cycle

CRAVINGS ☐   BACKACHE ☐   ENERGY 😊 😐 ☹️
ACNE ☐   HEADACHE ☐   MOOD 😊 😐 ☹️
CRAMPS ☐   SORE BREASTS ☐   SLEEP 😊 😐 ☹️

....
....
....

Day 6 of Cycle

CRAVINGS ☐   BACKACHE ☐   ENERGY 😊 😐 ☹️
ACNE ☐   HEADACHE ☐   MOOD 😊 😐 ☹️
CRAMPS ☐   SORE BREASTS ☐   SLEEP 😊 😐 ☹️

....
....
....

Day 7 of Cycle

CRAVINGS ☐   BACKACHE ☐   ENERGY 😊 😐 ☹️
ACNE ☐   HEADACHE ☐   MOOD 😊 😐 ☹️
CRAMPS ☐   SORE BREASTS ☐   SLEEP 😊 😐 ☹️

....
....
....

1	2	3	4	5	6	7	8	9	10	11	12
13	14	15	16	17	18	19	20	21	22	23	24
25	26	27	28	29	30	31	*Cross off dates that do not apply this month				

KEY: ■ HEAVY ◩ MEDIUM ◨ LIGHT ⊡ SPOTTING ⊠ N/A

_____ DAYS SINCE LAST PERIOD ♥ EXPECT NEXT PERIOD AROUND _____

Day 1 of Cycle

CRAVINGS ☐   BACKACHE ☐   ENERGY 😊 😐 🙁
ACNE ☐   HEADACHE ☐   MOOD 😊 😐 🙁
CRAMPS ☐   SORE BREASTS ☐   SLEEP 😊 😐 🙁

....
....
....

Day 2 of Cycle

CRAVINGS ☐   BACKACHE ☐   ENERGY 😊 😐 🙁
ACNE ☐   HEADACHE ☐   MOOD 😊 😐 🙁
CRAMPS ☐   SORE BREASTS ☐   SLEEP 😊 😐 🙁

....
....
....

Day 3 of Cycle

CRAVINGS ☐   BACKACHE ☐   ENERGY 😊 😐 🙁
ACNE ☐   HEADACHE ☐   MOOD 😊 😐 🙁
CRAMPS ☐   SORE BREASTS ☐   SLEEP 😊 😐 🙁

....
....
....

YEAR:_____

Day 4 of Cycle

CRAVINGS ☐   BACKACHE ☐   ENERGY 😀 😐 🙁
ACNE ☐   HEADACHE ☐   MOOD 😀 😐 🙁
CRAMPS ☐   SORE BREASTS ☐   SLEEP 😀 😐 🙁

....
....
....

Day 5 of Cycle

CRAVINGS ☐   BACKACHE ☐   ENERGY 😀 😐 🙁
ACNE ☐   HEADACHE ☐   MOOD 😀 😐 🙁
CRAMPS ☐   SORE BREASTS ☐   SLEEP 😀 😐 🙁

....
....
....

Day 6 of Cycle

CRAVINGS ☐   BACKACHE ☐   ENERGY 😀 😐 🙁
ACNE ☐   HEADACHE ☐   MOOD 😀 😐 🙁
CRAMPS ☐   SORE BREASTS ☐   SLEEP 😀 😐 🙁

....
....
....

Day 7 of Cycle

CRAVINGS ☐   BACKACHE ☐   ENERGY 😀 😐 🙁
ACNE ☐   HEADACHE ☐   MOOD 😀 😐 🙁
CRAMPS ☐   SORE BREASTS ☐   SLEEP 😀 😐 🙁

....
....
....

J	F	M	A	M	J	J	A	S	O	N	D

1	2	3	4	5	6	7	8	9	10	11	12
13	14	15	16	17	18	19	20	21	22	23	24
25	26	27	28	29	30	31	*Cross off dates that do not apply this month				

KEY: ◼ HEAVY ◢ MEDIUM ◹ LIGHT ⊡ SPOTTING ⊠ N/A

_____ DAYS SINCE LAST PERIOD ♥ EXPECT NEXT PERIOD AROUND _____

Day 1 of Cycle

CRAVINGS ☐   BACKACHE ☐   ENERGY ☺ 😐 ☹
ACNE ☐   HEADACHE ☐   MOOD ☺ 😐 ☹
CRAMPS ☐   SORE BREASTS ☐   SLEEP ☺ 😐 ☹

....
....
....

Day 2 of Cycle

CRAVINGS ☐   BACKACHE ☐   ENERGY ☺ 😐 ☹
ACNE ☐   HEADACHE ☐   MOOD ☺ 😐 ☹
CRAMPS ☐   SORE BREASTS ☐   SLEEP ☺ 😐 ☹

....
....
....

Day 3 of Cycle

CRAVINGS ☐   BACKACHE ☐   ENERGY ☺ 😐 ☹
ACNE ☐   HEADACHE ☐   MOOD ☺ 😐 ☹
CRAMPS ☐   SORE BREASTS ☐   SLEEP ☺ 😐 ☹

....
....
....

Day 4 of Cycle

CRAVINGS ☐   BACKACHE ☐   ENERGY 😃 😐 🙁
ACNE ☐   HEADACHE ☐   MOOD 😃 😐 🙁
CRAMPS ☐   SORE BREASTS ☐   SLEEP 😃 😐 🙁

....
....
....

Day 5 of Cycle

CRAVINGS ☐   BACKACHE ☐   ENERGY 😃 😐 🙁
ACNE ☐   HEADACHE ☐   MOOD 😃 😐 🙁
CRAMPS ☐   SORE BREASTS ☐   SLEEP 😃 😐 🙁

....
....
....

Day 6 of Cycle

CRAVINGS ☐   BACKACHE ☐   ENERGY 😃 😐 🙁
ACNE ☐   HEADACHE ☐   MOOD 😃 😐 🙁
CRAMPS ☐   SORE BREASTS ☐   SLEEP 😃 😐 🙁

....
....
....

Day 7 of Cycle

CRAVINGS ☐   BACKACHE ☐   ENERGY 😃 😐 🙁
ACNE ☐   HEADACHE ☐   MOOD 😃 😐 🙁
CRAMPS ☐   SORE BREASTS ☐   SLEEP 😃 😐 🙁

....
....
....

| J | F | m | A | m | J | J | A | S | O | N | D |

1	2	3	4	5	6	7	8	9	10	11	12
13	14	15	16	17	18	19	20	21	22	23	24
25	26	27	28	29	30	31	*Cross off dates that do not apply this month				

KEY: ■ HEAVY ◤ MEDIUM ◨ LIGHT • SPOTTING ⊠ N/A

_____ DAYS SINCE LAST PERIOD ♥ EXPECT NEXT PERIOD AROUND _____

Day 1 of Cycle

CRAVINGS ☐   BACKACHE ☐   ENERGY ☺ 😐 ☹
ACNE ☐   HEADACHE ☐   MOOD ☺ 😐 ☹
CRAMPS ☐   SORE BREASTS ☐   SLEEP ☺ 😐 ☹

....
....
....

Day 2 of Cycle

CRAVINGS ☐   BACKACHE ☐   ENERGY ☺ 😐 ☹
ACNE ☐   HEADACHE ☐   MOOD ☺ 😐 ☹
CRAMPS ☐   SORE BREASTS ☐   SLEEP ☺ 😐 ☹

....
....
....

Day 3 of Cycle

CRAVINGS ☐   BACKACHE ☐   ENERGY ☺ 😐 ☹
ACNE ☐   HEADACHE ☐   MOOD ☺ 😐 ☹
CRAMPS ☐   SORE BREASTS ☐   SLEEP ☺ 😐 ☹

....
....
....

Day 4 of Cycle

CRAVINGS ☐   BACKACHE ☐   ENERGY 😊 😐 ☹️
ACNE ☐   HEADACHE ☐   MOOD 😊 😐 ☹️
CRAMPS ☐   SORE BREASTS ☐   SLEEP 😊 😐 ☹️

....
....
....

Day 5 of Cycle

CRAVINGS ☐   BACKACHE ☐   ENERGY 😊 😐 ☹️
ACNE ☐   HEADACHE ☐   MOOD 😊 😐 ☹️
CRAMPS ☐   SORE BREASTS ☐   SLEEP 😊 😐 ☹️

....
....
....

Day 6 of Cycle

CRAVINGS ☐   BACKACHE ☐   ENERGY 😊 😐 ☹️
ACNE ☐   HEADACHE ☐   MOOD 😊 😐 ☹️
CRAMPS ☐   SORE BREASTS ☐   SLEEP 😊 😐 ☹️

....
....
....

Day 7 of Cycle

CRAVINGS ☐   BACKACHE ☐   ENERGY 😊 😐 ☹️
ACNE ☐   HEADACHE ☐   MOOD 😊 😐 ☹️
CRAMPS ☐   SORE BREASTS ☐   SLEEP 😊 😐 ☹️

....
....
....

J	F	M	A	M	J	J	A	S	O	N	D

1	2	3	4	5	6	7	8	9	10	11	12
13	14	15	16	17	18	19	20	21	22	23	24
25	26	27	28	29	30	31	*Cross off dates that do not apply this month				

KEY: ■ HEAVY ◢ MEDIUM ⧄ LIGHT • SPOTTING ⊠ N/A

_____ DAYS SINCE LAST PERIOD ♥ EXPECT NEXT PERIOD AROUND _____

Day 1 of Cycle

CRAVINGS ☐   BACKACHE ☐   ENERGY 😊 😐 ☹
ACNE ☐   HEADACHE ☐   MOOD 😊 😐 ☹
CRAMPS ☐   SORE BREASTS ☐   SLEEP 😊 😐 ☹

....
....
....

Day 2 of Cycle

CRAVINGS ☐   BACKACHE ☐   ENERGY 😊 😐 ☹
ACNE ☐   HEADACHE ☐   MOOD 😊 😐 ☹
CRAMPS ☐   SORE BREASTS ☐   SLEEP 😊 😐 ☹

....
....
....

Day 3 of Cycle

CRAVINGS ☐   BACKACHE ☐   ENERGY 😊 😐 ☹
ACNE ☐   HEADACHE ☐   MOOD 😊 😐 ☹
CRAMPS ☐   SORE BREASTS ☐   SLEEP 😊 😐 ☹

....
....
....

Day 4 of Cycle

CRAVINGS ☐   BACKACHE ☐   ENERGY 😊 😐 ☹
ACNE ☐   HEADACHE ☐   MOOD 😊 😐 ☹
CRAMPS ☐   SORE BREASTS ☐   SLEEP 😊 😐 ☹

....
....
....

Day 5 of Cycle

CRAVINGS ☐   BACKACHE ☐   ENERGY 😊 😐 ☹
ACNE ☐   HEADACHE ☐   MOOD 😊 😐 ☹
CRAMPS ☐   SORE BREASTS ☐   SLEEP 😊 😐 ☹

....
....
....

Day 6 of Cycle

CRAVINGS ☐   BACKACHE ☐   ENERGY 😊 😐 ☹
ACNE ☐   HEADACHE ☐   MOOD 😊 😐 ☹
CRAMPS ☐   SORE BREASTS ☐   SLEEP 😊 😐 ☹

....
....
....

Day 7 of Cycle

CRAVINGS ☐   BACKACHE ☐   ENERGY 😊 😐 ☹
ACNE ☐   HEADACHE ☐   MOOD 😊 😐 ☹
CRAMPS ☐   SORE BREASTS ☐   SLEEP 😊 😐 ☹

....
....
....

| J | F | M | A | M | J | J | A | S | O | N | D |

1	2	3	4	5	6	7	8	9	10	11	12
13	14	15	16	17	18	19	20	21	22	23	24
25	26	27	28	29	30	31	*Cross off dates that do not apply this month				

KEY: ■ HEAVY ◢ MEDIUM ⧄ LIGHT ⊡ SPOTTING ⊠ N/A

_____ DAYS SINCE LAST PERIOD ♥ EXPECT NEXT PERIOD AROUND _____

Day 1 of Cycle

CRAVINGS ☐   BACKACHE ☐   ENERGY ☺ 😐 ☹
ACNE ☐   HEADACHE ☐   MOOD ☺ 😐 ☹
CRAMPS ☐   SORE BREASTS ☐   SLEEP ☺ 😐 ☹

....
....
....

Day 2 of Cycle

CRAVINGS ☐   BACKACHE ☐   ENERGY ☺ 😐 ☹
ACNE ☐   HEADACHE ☐   MOOD ☺ 😐 ☹
CRAMPS ☐   SORE BREASTS ☐   SLEEP ☺ 😐 ☹

....
....
....

Day 3 of Cycle

CRAVINGS ☐   BACKACHE ☐   ENERGY ☺ 😐 ☹
ACNE ☐   HEADACHE ☐   MOOD ☺ 😐 ☹
CRAMPS ☐   SORE BREASTS ☐   SLEEP ☺ 😐 ☹

....
....
....

Day 4 of Cycle

CRAVINGS ☐   BACKACHE ☐   ENERGY 😊 😐 ☹️
ACNE ☐   HEADACHE ☐   MOOD 😊 😐 ☹️
CRAMPS ☐   SORE BREASTS ☐   SLEEP 😊 😐 ☹️

....
....
....

Day 5 of Cycle

CRAVINGS ☐   BACKACHE ☐   ENERGY 😊 😐 ☹️
ACNE ☐   HEADACHE ☐   MOOD 😊 😐 ☹️
CRAMPS ☐   SORE BREASTS ☐   SLEEP 😊 😐 ☹️

....
....
....

Day 6 of Cycle

CRAVINGS ☐   BACKACHE ☐   ENERGY 😊 😐 ☹️
ACNE ☐   HEADACHE ☐   MOOD 😊 😐 ☹️
CRAMPS ☐   SORE BREASTS ☐   SLEEP 😊 😐 ☹️

....
....
....

Day 7 of Cycle

CRAVINGS ☐   BACKACHE ☐   ENERGY 😊 😐 ☹️
ACNE ☐   HEADACHE ☐   MOOD 😊 😐 ☹️
CRAMPS ☐   SORE BREASTS ☐   SLEEP 😊 😐 ☹️

....
....
....

J	F	M	A	M	J	J	A	S	O	N	D
1	2	3	4	5	6	7	8	9	10	11	12
13	14	15	16	17	18	19	20	21	22	23	24
25	26	27	28	29	30	31	*Cross off dates that do not apply this month				

KEY: ■ HEAVY ◪ MEDIUM ◫ LIGHT ● SPOTTING ⊠ N/A

_____ DAYS SINCE LAST PERIOD ♥ EXPECT NEXT PERIOD AROUND _____

Day 1 of Cycle

CRAVINGS ☐   BACKACHE ☐   ENERGY 😊 😐 🙁
ACNE ☐   HEADACHE ☐   MOOD 😊 😐 🙁
CRAMPS ☐   SORE BREASTS ☐   SLEEP 😊 😐 🙁

....
....
....

Day 2 of Cycle

CRAVINGS ☐   BACKACHE ☐   ENERGY 😊 😐 🙁
ACNE ☐   HEADACHE ☐   MOOD 😊 😐 🙁
CRAMPS ☐   SORE BREASTS ☐   SLEEP 😊 😐 🙁

....
....
....

Day 3 of Cycle

CRAVINGS ☐   BACKACHE ☐   ENERGY 😊 😐 🙁
ACNE ☐   HEADACHE ☐   MOOD 😊 😐 🙁
CRAMPS ☐   SORE BREASTS ☐   SLEEP 😊 😐 🙁

....
....
....

Day 4 of Cycle

CRAVINGS ☐   BACKACHE ☐   ENERGY 😊 😐 😟
ACNE ☐   HEADACHE ☐   MOOD 😊 😐 😟
CRAMPS ☐   SORE BREASTS ☐   SLEEP 😊 😐 😟

....
....
....

Day 5 of Cycle

CRAVINGS ☐   BACKACHE ☐   ENERGY 😊 😐 😟
ACNE ☐   HEADACHE ☐   MOOD 😊 😐 😟
CRAMPS ☐   SORE BREASTS ☐   SLEEP 😊 😐 😟

....
....
....

Day 6 of Cycle

CRAVINGS ☐   BACKACHE ☐   ENERGY 😊 😐 😟
ACNE ☐   HEADACHE ☐   MOOD 😊 😐 😟
CRAMPS ☐   SORE BREASTS ☐   SLEEP 😊 😐 😟

....
....
....

Day 7 of Cycle

CRAVINGS ☐   BACKACHE ☐   ENERGY 😊 😐 😟
ACNE ☐   HEADACHE ☐   MOOD 😊 😐 😟
CRAMPS ☐   SORE BREASTS ☐   SLEEP 😊 😐 😟

....
....
....

| J | F | M | A | M | J | J | A | S | O | N | D |

1	2	3	4	5	6	7	8	9	10	11	12
13	14	15	16	17	18	19	20	21	22	23	24
25	26	27	28	29	30	31	*Cross off dates that do not apply this month				

KEY: ■ HEAVY ◤ MEDIUM ◩ LIGHT • SPOTTING ⊠ N/A

_____ DAYS SINCE LAST PERIOD ♥ EXPECT NEXT PERIOD AROUND _____

Day 1 of Cycle

CRAVINGS ☐   BACKACHE ☐   ENERGY ☺ 😐 ☹
ACNE ☐   HEADACHE ☐   MOOD ☺ 😐 ☹
CRAMPS ☐   SORE BREASTS ☐   SLEEP ☺ 😐 ☹

....
....
....

Day 2 of Cycle

CRAVINGS ☐   BACKACHE ☐   ENERGY ☺ 😐 ☹
ACNE ☐   HEADACHE ☐   MOOD ☺ 😐 ☹
CRAMPS ☐   SORE BREASTS ☐   SLEEP ☺ 😐 ☹

....
....
....

Day 3 of Cycle

CRAVINGS ☐   BACKACHE ☐   ENERGY ☺ 😐 ☹
ACNE ☐   HEADACHE ☐   MOOD ☺ 😐 ☹
CRAMPS ☐   SORE BREASTS ☐   SLEEP ☺ 😐 ☹

....
....
....

YEAR:_____

Day 4 of Cycle

CRAVINGS ☐   BACKACHE ☐   ENERGY 🙂 😐 🙁
ACNE ☐   HEADACHE ☐   MOOD 🙂 😐 🙁
CRAMPS ☐   SORE BREASTS ☐   SLEEP 🙂 😐 🙁

....
....
....

Day 5 of Cycle

CRAVINGS ☐   BACKACHE ☐   ENERGY 🙂 😐 🙁
ACNE ☐   HEADACHE ☐   MOOD 🙂 😐 🙁
CRAMPS ☐   SORE BREASTS ☐   SLEEP 🙂 😐 🙁

....
....
....

Day 6 of Cycle

CRAVINGS ☐   BACKACHE ☐   ENERGY 🙂 😐 🙁
ACNE ☐   HEADACHE ☐   MOOD 🙂 😐 🙁
CRAMPS ☐   SORE BREASTS ☐   SLEEP 🙂 😐 🙁

....
....
....

Day 7 of Cycle

CRAVINGS ☐   BACKACHE ☐   ENERGY 🙂 😐 🙁
ACNE ☐   HEADACHE ☐   MOOD 🙂 😐 🙁
CRAMPS ☐   SORE BREASTS ☐   SLEEP 🙂 😐 🙁

....
....
....

1	2	3	4	5	6	7	8	9	10	11	12
13	14	15	16	17	18	19	20	21	22	23	24
25	26	27	28	29	30	31	*Cross off dates that do not apply this month				

KEY: ■ HEAVY ◤ MEDIUM ▧ LIGHT • SPOTTING ⊠ N/A

_____ DAYS SINCE LAST PERIOD ♥ EXPECT NEXT PERIOD AROUND _____

Day 1 of Cycle

CRAVINGS ☐   BACKACHE ☐   ENERGY 😃 😐 ☹
ACNE ☐   HEADACHE ☐   MOOD 😃 😐 ☹
CRAMPS ☐   SORE BREASTS ☐   SLEEP 😃 😐 ☹

....
....
....

Day 2 of Cycle

CRAVINGS ☐   BACKACHE ☐   ENERGY 😃 😐 ☹
ACNE ☐   HEADACHE ☐   MOOD 😃 😐 ☹
CRAMPS ☐   SORE BREASTS ☐   SLEEP 😃 😐 ☹

....
....
....

Day 3 of Cycle

CRAVINGS ☐   BACKACHE ☐   ENERGY 😃 😐 ☹
ACNE ☐   HEADACHE ☐   MOOD 😃 😐 ☹
CRAMPS ☐   SORE BREASTS ☐   SLEEP 😃 😐 ☹

....
....
....

Day 4 of Cycle

CRAVINGS ☐   BACKACHE ☐   ENERGY ☺ 😐 ☹
ACNE ☐   HEADACHE ☐   MOOD ☺ 😐 ☹
CRAMPS ☐   SORE BREASTS ☐   SLEEP ☺ 😐 ☹

....
....
....

Day 5 of Cycle

CRAVINGS ☐   BACKACHE ☐   ENERGY ☺ 😐 ☹
ACNE ☐   HEADACHE ☐   MOOD ☺ 😐 ☹
CRAMPS ☐   SORE BREASTS ☐   SLEEP ☺ 😐 ☹

....
....
....

Day 6 of Cycle

CRAVINGS ☐   BACKACHE ☐   ENERGY ☺ 😐 ☹
ACNE ☐   HEADACHE ☐   MOOD ☺ 😐 ☹
CRAMPS ☐   SORE BREASTS ☐   SLEEP ☺ 😐 ☹

....
....
....

Day 7 of Cycle

CRAVINGS ☐   BACKACHE ☐   ENERGY ☺ 😐 ☹
ACNE ☐   HEADACHE ☐   MOOD ☺ 😐 ☹
CRAMPS ☐   SORE BREASTS ☐   SLEEP ☺ 😐 ☹

....
....
....

| J | F | M | A | M | J | J | A | S | O | N | D |

1	2	3	4	5	6	7	8	9	10	11	12
13	14	15	16	17	18	19	20	21	22	23	24
25	26	27	28	29	30	31	*Cross off dates that do not apply this month				

KEY: ■ HEAVY ◢ MEDIUM ▨ LIGHT ● SPOTTING ⊠ N/A

_____ DAYS SINCE LAST PERIOD ♥ EXPECT NEXT PERIOD AROUND _____

Day 1 of Cycle

CRAVINGS ☐   BACKACHE ☐   ENERGY 😄 😐 🙁
ACNE ☐   HEADACHE ☐   MOOD 😄 😐 🙁
CRAMPS ☐   SORE BREASTS ☐   SLEEP 😄 😐 🙁

....
....
....

Day 2 of Cycle

CRAVINGS ☐   BACKACHE ☐   ENERGY 😄 😐 🙁
ACNE ☐   HEADACHE ☐   MOOD 😄 😐 🙁
CRAMPS ☐   SORE BREASTS ☐   SLEEP 😄 😐 🙁

....
....
....

Day 3 of Cycle

CRAVINGS ☐   BACKACHE ☐   ENERGY 😄 😐 🙁
ACNE ☐   HEADACHE ☐   MOOD 😄 😐 🙁
CRAMPS ☐   SORE BREASTS ☐   SLEEP 😄 😐 🙁

....
....
....

Day 4 of Cycle

CRAVINGS ☐   BACKACHE ☐   ENERGY 😃 😐 ☹
ACNE ☐   HEADACHE ☐   MOOD 😃 😐 ☹
CRAMPS ☐   SORE BREASTS ☐   SLEEP 😃 😐 ☹

....
....
....

Day 5 of Cycle

CRAVINGS ☐   BACKACHE ☐   ENERGY 😃 😐 ☹
ACNE ☐   HEADACHE ☐   MOOD 😃 😐 ☹
CRAMPS ☐   SORE BREASTS ☐   SLEEP 😃 😐 ☹

....
....
....

Day 6 of Cycle

CRAVINGS ☐   BACKACHE ☐   ENERGY 😃 😐 ☹
ACNE ☐   HEADACHE ☐   MOOD 😃 😐 ☹
CRAMPS ☐   SORE BREASTS ☐   SLEEP 😃 😐 ☹

....
....
....

Day 7 of Cycle

CRAVINGS ☐   BACKACHE ☐   ENERGY 😃 😐 ☹
ACNE ☐   HEADACHE ☐   MOOD 😃 😐 ☹
CRAMPS ☐   SORE BREASTS ☐   SLEEP 😃 😐 ☹

....
....
....

J	F	M	A	M	J	J	A	S	O	N	D

1	2	3	4	5	6	7	8	9	10	11	12
13	14	15	16	17	18	19	20	21	22	23	24
25	26	27	28	29	30	31	*Cross off dates that do not apply this month				

KEY: ■ HEAVY ◢ MEDIUM ◩ LIGHT ⊡ SPOTTING ⊠ N/A

_____ DAYS SINCE LAST PERIOD ♥ EXPECT NEXT PERIOD AROUND _____

Day 1 of Cycle

CRAVINGS ☐   BACKACHE ☐   ENERGY ☻ ☺ ☹
ACNE ☐   HEADACHE ☐   MOOD ☻ ☺ ☹
CRAMPS ☐   SORE BREASTS ☐   SLEEP ☻ ☺ ☹

....
....
....

Day 2 of Cycle

CRAVINGS ☐   BACKACHE ☐   ENERGY ☻ ☺ ☹
ACNE ☐   HEADACHE ☐   MOOD ☻ ☺ ☹
CRAMPS ☐   SORE BREASTS ☐   SLEEP ☻ ☺ ☹

....
....
....

Day 3 of Cycle

CRAVINGS ☐   BACKACHE ☐   ENERGY ☻ ☺ ☹
ACNE ☐   HEADACHE ☐   MOOD ☻ ☺ ☹
CRAMPS ☐   SORE BREASTS ☐   SLEEP ☻ ☺ ☹

....
....
....

Day 4 of Cycle

CRAVINGS ☐   BACKACHE ☐   ENERGY 😄 😐 😞
ACNE ☐   HEADACHE ☐   MOOD 😄 😐 😞
CRAMPS ☐   SORE BREASTS ☐   SLEEP 😄 😐 😞

....
....
....

Day 5 of Cycle

CRAVINGS ☐   BACKACHE ☐   ENERGY 😄 😐 😞
ACNE ☐   HEADACHE ☐   MOOD 😄 😐 😞
CRAMPS ☐   SORE BREASTS ☐   SLEEP 😄 😐 😞

....
....
....

Day 6 of Cycle

CRAVINGS ☐   BACKACHE ☐   ENERGY 😄 😐 😞
ACNE ☐   HEADACHE ☐   MOOD 😄 😐 😞
CRAMPS ☐   SORE BREASTS ☐   SLEEP 😄 😐 😞

....
....
....

Day 7 of Cycle

CRAVINGS ☐   BACKACHE ☐   ENERGY 😄 😐 😞
ACNE ☐   HEADACHE ☐   MOOD 😄 😐 😞
CRAMPS ☐   SORE BREASTS ☐   SLEEP 😄 😐 😞

....
....
....

1	2	3	4	5	6	7	8	9	10	11	12
13	14	15	16	17	18	19	20	21	22	23	24
25	26	27	28	29	30	31	*Cross off dates that do not apply this month				

KEY: ■ HEAVY ◢ MEDIUM ◩ LIGHT ⦿ SPOTTING ⊠ N/A

_____ DAYS SINCE LAST PERIOD ♥ EXPECT NEXT PERIOD AROUND _____

Day 1 of Cycle

CRAVINGS ☐   BACKACHE ☐   ENERGY ☺ 😐 ☹
ACNE ☐   HEADACHE ☐   MOOD ☺ 😐 ☹
CRAMPS ☐   SORE BREASTS ☐   SLEEP ☺ 😐 ☹

....
....
....

Day 2 of Cycle

CRAVINGS ☐   BACKACHE ☐   ENERGY ☺ 😐 ☹
ACNE ☐   HEADACHE ☐   MOOD ☺ 😐 ☹
CRAMPS ☐   SORE BREASTS ☐   SLEEP ☺ 😐 ☹

....
....
....

Day 3 of Cycle

CRAVINGS ☐   BACKACHE ☐   ENERGY ☺ 😐 ☹
ACNE ☐   HEADACHE ☐   MOOD ☺ 😐 ☹
CRAMPS ☐   SORE BREASTS ☐   SLEEP ☺ 😐 ☹

....
....
....

Day 4 of Cycle

CRAVINGS ☐   BACKACHE ☐   ENERGY 🙂 😐 ☹️
ACNE ☐   HEADACHE ☐   MOOD 🙂 😐 ☹️
CRAMPS ☐   SORE BREASTS ☐   SLEEP 🙂 😐 ☹️

....
....
....

Day 5 of Cycle

CRAVINGS ☐   BACKACHE ☐   ENERGY 🙂 😐 ☹️
ACNE ☐   HEADACHE ☐   MOOD 🙂 😐 ☹️
CRAMPS ☐   SORE BREASTS ☐   SLEEP 🙂 😐 ☹️

....
....
....

Day 6 of Cycle

CRAVINGS ☐   BACKACHE ☐   ENERGY 🙂 😐 ☹️
ACNE ☐   HEADACHE ☐   MOOD 🙂 😐 ☹️
CRAMPS ☐   SORE BREASTS ☐   SLEEP 🙂 😐 ☹️

....
....
....

Day 7 of Cycle

CRAVINGS ☐   BACKACHE ☐   ENERGY 🙂 😐 ☹️
ACNE ☐   HEADACHE ☐   MOOD 🙂 😐 ☹️
CRAMPS ☐   SORE BREASTS ☐   SLEEP 🙂 😐 ☹️

....
....
....

J	F	M	A	M	J	J	A	S	O	N	D

1	2	3	4	5	6	7	8	9	10	11	12
13	14	15	16	17	18	19	20	21	22	23	24
25	26	27	28	29	30	31	*Cross off dates that do not apply this month				

KEY: ■ HEAVY ◤ MEDIUM ◩ LIGHT ⊡ SPOTTING ⊠ N/A

_____ DAYS SINCE LAST PERIOD ♥ EXPECT NEXT PERIOD AROUND _____

Day 1 of Cycle

CRAVINGS ☐   BACKACHE ☐   ENERGY ☺ ☺ ☹
ACNE ☐   HEADACHE ☐   MOOD ☺ ☺ ☹
CRAMPS ☐   SORE BREASTS ☐   SLEEP ☺ ☺ ☹

....
....
....

Day 2 of Cycle

CRAVINGS ☐   BACKACHE ☐   ENERGY ☺ ☺ ☹
ACNE ☐   HEADACHE ☐   MOOD ☺ ☺ ☹
CRAMPS ☐   SORE BREASTS ☐   SLEEP ☺ ☺ ☹

....
....
....

Day 3 of Cycle

CRAVINGS ☐   BACKACHE ☐   ENERGY ☺ ☺ ☹
ACNE ☐   HEADACHE ☐   MOOD ☺ ☺ ☹
CRAMPS ☐   SORE BREASTS ☐   SLEEP ☺ ☺ ☹

....
....
....

Day 4 of Cycle

CRAVINGS ☐   BACKACHE ☐   ENERGY 😃 😐 ☹
ACNE ☐   HEADACHE ☐   MOOD 😃 😐 ☹
CRAMPS ☐   SORE BREASTS ☐   SLEEP 😃 😐 ☹

....
....
....

Day 5 of Cycle

CRAVINGS ☐   BACKACHE ☐   ENERGY 😃 😐 ☹
ACNE ☐   HEADACHE ☐   MOOD 😃 😐 ☹
CRAMPS ☐   SORE BREASTS ☐   SLEEP 😃 😐 ☹

....
....
....

Day 6 of Cycle

CRAVINGS ☐   BACKACHE ☐   ENERGY 😃 😐 ☹
ACNE ☐   HEADACHE ☐   MOOD 😃 😐 ☹
CRAMPS ☐   SORE BREASTS ☐   SLEEP 😃 😐 ☹

....
....
....

Day 7 of Cycle

CRAVINGS ☐   BACKACHE ☐   ENERGY 😃 😐 ☹
ACNE ☐   HEADACHE ☐   MOOD 😃 😐 ☹
CRAMPS ☐   SORE BREASTS ☐   SLEEP 😃 😐 ☹

....
....
....

J	F	M	A	M	J	J	A	S	O	N	D

1	2	3	4	5	6	7	8	9	10	11	12
13	14	15	16	17	18	19	20	21	22	23	24
25	26	27	28	29	30	31	*Cross off dates that do not apply this month				

KEY: ■ HEAVY ◩ MEDIUM ▨ LIGHT ⊡ SPOTTING ⊠ N/A

_____ DAYS SINCE LAST PERIOD ♥ EXPECT NEXT PERIOD AROUND _____

Day 1 of Cycle

CRAVINGS ☐   BACKACHE ☐   ENERGY ☺ 😐 ☹
ACNE ☐   HEADACHE ☐   MOOD ☺ 😐 ☹
CRAMPS ☐   SORE BREASTS ☐   SLEEP ☺ 😐 ☹

....
....
....

Day 2 of Cycle

CRAVINGS ☐   BACKACHE ☐   ENERGY ☺ 😐 ☹
ACNE ☐   HEADACHE ☐   MOOD ☺ 😐 ☹
CRAMPS ☐   SORE BREASTS ☐   SLEEP ☺ 😐 ☹

....
....
....

Day 3 of Cycle

CRAVINGS ☐   BACKACHE ☐   ENERGY ☺ 😐 ☹
ACNE ☐   HEADACHE ☐   MOOD ☺ 😐 ☹
CRAMPS ☐   SORE BREASTS ☐   SLEEP ☺ 😐 ☹

....
....
....

Day 4 of Cycle

CRAVINGS ☐   BACKACHE ☐   ENERGY 😊 😐 😞
ACNE ☐   HEADACHE ☐   MOOD 😊 😐 😞
CRAMPS ☐   SORE BREASTS ☐   SLEEP 😊 😐 😞

....
....
....

Day 5 of Cycle

CRAVINGS ☐   BACKACHE ☐   ENERGY 😊 😐 😞
ACNE ☐   HEADACHE ☐   MOOD 😊 😐 😞
CRAMPS ☐   SORE BREASTS ☐   SLEEP 😊 😐 😞

....
....
....

Day 6 of Cycle

CRAVINGS ☐   BACKACHE ☐   ENERGY 😊 😐 😞
ACNE ☐   HEADACHE ☐   MOOD 😊 😐 😞
CRAMPS ☐   SORE BREASTS ☐   SLEEP 😊 😐 😞

....
....
....

Day 7 of Cycle

CRAVINGS ☐   BACKACHE ☐   ENERGY 😊 😐 😞
ACNE ☐   HEADACHE ☐   MOOD 😊 😐 😞
CRAMPS ☐   SORE BREASTS ☐   SLEEP 😊 😐 😞

....
....
....

J	F	M	A	M	J	J	A	S	O	N	D

1	2	3	4	5	6	7	8	9	10	11	12
13	14	15	16	17	18	19	20	21	22	23	24
25	26	27	28	29	30	31	*Cross off dates that do not apply this month				

KEY: ■ HEAVY ◤ MEDIUM ◩ LIGHT • SPOTTING ☒ N/A

_____ DAYS SINCE LAST PERIOD ♥ EXPECT NEXT PERIOD AROUND _____

Day 1 of Cycle

CRAVINGS ☐   BACKACHE ☐   ENERGY 😊 😐 ☹
ACNE ☐   HEADACHE ☐   MOOD 😊 😐 ☹
CRAMPS ☐   SORE BREASTS ☐   SLEEP 😊 😐 ☹

....
....
....

Day 2 of Cycle

CRAVINGS ☐   BACKACHE ☐   ENERGY 😊 😐 ☹
ACNE ☐   HEADACHE ☐   MOOD 😊 😐 ☹
CRAMPS ☐   SORE BREASTS ☐   SLEEP 😊 😐 ☹

....
....
....

Day 3 of Cycle

CRAVINGS ☐   BACKACHE ☐   ENERGY 😊 😐 ☹
ACNE ☐   HEADACHE ☐   MOOD 😊 😐 ☹
CRAMPS ☐   SORE BREASTS ☐   SLEEP 😊 😐 ☹

....
....
....

Day 4 of Cycle

CRAVINGS ☐   BACKACHE ☐   ENERGY 😄 😐 🙁
ACNE ☐   HEADACHE ☐   MOOD 😄 😐 🙁
CRAMPS ☐   SORE BREASTS ☐   SLEEP 😄 😐 🙁

....
....
....

Day 5 of Cycle

CRAVINGS ☐   BACKACHE ☐   ENERGY 😄 😐 🙁
ACNE ☐   HEADACHE ☐   MOOD 😄 😐 🙁
CRAMPS ☐   SORE BREASTS ☐   SLEEP 😄 😐 🙁

....
....
....

Day 6 of Cycle

CRAVINGS ☐   BACKACHE ☐   ENERGY 😄 😐 🙁
ACNE ☐   HEADACHE ☐   MOOD 😄 😐 🙁
CRAMPS ☐   SORE BREASTS ☐   SLEEP 😄 😐 🙁

....
....
....

Day 7 of Cycle

CRAVINGS ☐   BACKACHE ☐   ENERGY 😄 😐 🙁
ACNE ☐   HEADACHE ☐   MOOD 😄 😐 🙁
CRAMPS ☐   SORE BREASTS ☐   SLEEP 😄 😐 🙁

....
....
....

J	F	m	A	m	J	J	A	S	O	N	D

1	2	3	4	5	6	7	8	9	10	11	12
13	14	15	16	17	18	19	20	21	22	23	24
25	26	27	28	29	30	31	*Cross off dates that do not apply this month				

KEY: ■ HEAVY ◤ MEDIUM ◩ LIGHT ⊡ SPOTTING ⊠ N/A

_____ DAYS SINCE LAST PERIOD ♥ EXPECT NEXT PERIOD AROUND _____

Day 1 of Cycle

CRAVINGS ☐   BACKACHE ☐   ENERGY 😃 😐 ☹
ACNE ☐   HEADACHE ☐   MOOD 😃 😐 ☹
CRAMPS ☐   SORE BREASTS ☐   SLEEP 😃 😐 ☹

....
....
....

Day 2 of Cycle

CRAVINGS ☐   BACKACHE ☐   ENERGY 😃 😐 ☹
ACNE ☐   HEADACHE ☐   MOOD 😃 😐 ☹
CRAMPS ☐   SORE BREASTS ☐   SLEEP 😃 😐 ☹

....
....
....

Day 3 of Cycle

CRAVINGS ☐   BACKACHE ☐   ENERGY 😃 😐 ☹
ACNE ☐   HEADACHE ☐   MOOD 😃 😐 ☹
CRAMPS ☐   SORE BREASTS ☐   SLEEP 😃 😐 ☹

....
....
....

YEAR:_____

Day 4 of Cycle

CRAVINGS ☐   BACKACHE ☐   ENERGY 😃 😐 😟
ACNE ☐   HEADACHE ☐   MOOD 😃 😐 😟
CRAMPS ☐   SORE BREASTS ☐   SLEEP 😃 😐 😟

....
....
....

Day 5 of Cycle

CRAVINGS ☐   BACKACHE ☐   ENERGY 😃 😐 😟
ACNE ☐   HEADACHE ☐   MOOD 😃 😐 😟
CRAMPS ☐   SORE BREASTS ☐   SLEEP 😃 😐 😟

....
....
....

Day 6 of Cycle

CRAVINGS ☐   BACKACHE ☐   ENERGY 😃 😐 😟
ACNE ☐   HEADACHE ☐   MOOD 😃 😐 😟
CRAMPS ☐   SORE BREASTS ☐   SLEEP 😃 😐 😟

....
....
....

Day 7 of Cycle

CRAVINGS ☐   BACKACHE ☐   ENERGY 😃 😐 😟
ACNE ☐   HEADACHE ☐   MOOD 😃 😐 😟
CRAMPS ☐   SORE BREASTS ☐   SLEEP 😃 😐 😟

....
....
....

J	F	M	A	M	J	J	A	S	O	N	D

1	2	3	4	5	6	7	8	9	10	11	12
13	14	15	16	17	18	19	20	21	22	23	24
25	26	27	28	29	30	31	*Cross off dates that do not apply this month				

KEY: ■ HEAVY ◪ MEDIUM ◹ LIGHT ● SPOTTING ⊠ N/A

_____ DAYS SINCE LAST PERIOD ♥ EXPECT NEXT PERIOD AROUND _____

Day 1 of Cycle

CRAVINGS ☐   BACKACHE ☐   ENERGY 😀 😐 ☹
ACNE ☐   HEADACHE ☐   MOOD 😀 😐 ☹
CRAMPS ☐   SORE BREASTS ☐   SLEEP 😀 😐 ☹

....
....
....

Day 2 of Cycle

CRAVINGS ☐   BACKACHE ☐   ENERGY 😀 😐 ☹
ACNE ☐   HEADACHE ☐   MOOD 😀 😐 ☹
CRAMPS ☐   SORE BREASTS ☐   SLEEP 😀 😐 ☹

....
....
....

Day 3 of Cycle

CRAVINGS ☐   BACKACHE ☐   ENERGY 😀 😐 ☹
ACNE ☐   HEADACHE ☐   MOOD 😀 😐 ☹
CRAMPS ☐   SORE BREASTS ☐   SLEEP 😀 😐 ☹

....
....
....

Day 4 of Cycle

CRAVINGS ☐   BACKACHE ☐   ENERGY 😀 😐 🙁
ACNE ☐   HEADACHE ☐   MOOD 😀 😐 🙁
CRAMPS ☐   SORE BREASTS ☐   SLEEP 😀 😐 🙁

....
....
....

Day 5 of Cycle

CRAVINGS ☐   BACKACHE ☐   ENERGY 😀 😐 🙁
ACNE ☐   HEADACHE ☐   MOOD 😀 😐 🙁
CRAMPS ☐   SORE BREASTS ☐   SLEEP 😀 😐 🙁

....
....
....

Day 6 of Cycle

CRAVINGS ☐   BACKACHE ☐   ENERGY 😀 😐 🙁
ACNE ☐   HEADACHE ☐   MOOD 😀 😐 🙁
CRAMPS ☐   SORE BREASTS ☐   SLEEP 😀 😐 🙁

....
....
....

Day 7 of Cycle

CRAVINGS ☐   BACKACHE ☐   ENERGY 😀 😐 🙁
ACNE ☐   HEADACHE ☐   MOOD 😀 😐 🙁
CRAMPS ☐   SORE BREASTS ☐   SLEEP 😀 😐 🙁

....
....
....

J F m A m J J A S O N D

1	2	3	4	5	6	7	8	9	10	11	12
13	14	15	16	17	18	19	20	21	22	23	24
25	26	27	28	29	30	31	*Cross off dates that do not apply this month				

KEY: ■ HEAVY ◪ MEDIUM ◫ LIGHT ● SPOTTING ⊠ N/A

_____ DAYS SINCE LAST PERIOD ♥ EXPECT NEXT PERIOD AROUND _____

Day 1 of Cycle

CRAVINGS ☐   BACKACHE ☐   ENERGY ☺ 😐 ☹
ACNE ☐   HEADACHE ☐   MOOD ☺ 😐 ☹
CRAMPS ☐   SORE BREASTS ☐   SLEEP ☺ 😐 ☹

....
....
....

Day 2 of Cycle

CRAVINGS ☐   BACKACHE ☐   ENERGY ☺ 😐 ☹
ACNE ☐   HEADACHE ☐   MOOD ☺ 😐 ☹
CRAMPS ☐   SORE BREASTS ☐   SLEEP ☺ 😐 ☹

....
....
....

Day 3 of Cycle

CRAVINGS ☐   BACKACHE ☐   ENERGY ☺ 😐 ☹
ACNE ☐   HEADACHE ☐   MOOD ☺ 😐 ☹
CRAMPS ☐   SORE BREASTS ☐   SLEEP ☺ 😐 ☹

....
....
....

Day 4 of Cycle

CRAVINGS ☐   BACKACHE ☐   ENERGY 😊 😐 ☹️
ACNE ☐   HEADACHE ☐   MOOD 😊 😐 ☹️
CRAMPS ☐   SORE BREASTS ☐   SLEEP 😊 😐 ☹️

....
....
....

Day 5 of Cycle

CRAVINGS ☐   BACKACHE ☐   ENERGY 😊 😐 ☹️
ACNE ☐   HEADACHE ☐   MOOD 😊 😐 ☹️
CRAMPS ☐   SORE BREASTS ☐   SLEEP 😊 😐 ☹️

....
....
....

Day 6 of Cycle

CRAVINGS ☐   BACKACHE ☐   ENERGY 😊 😐 ☹️
ACNE ☐   HEADACHE ☐   MOOD 😊 😐 ☹️
CRAMPS ☐   SORE BREASTS ☐   SLEEP 😊 😐 ☹️

....
....
....

Day 7 of Cycle

CRAVINGS ☐   BACKACHE ☐   ENERGY 😊 😐 ☹️
ACNE ☐   HEADACHE ☐   MOOD 😊 😐 ☹️
CRAMPS ☐   SORE BREASTS ☐   SLEEP 😊 😐 ☹️

....
....
....

J	F	M	A	M	J	J	A	S	O	N	D

1	2	3	4	5	6	7	8	9	10	11	12
13	14	15	16	17	18	19	20	21	22	23	24
25	26	27	28	29	30	31	*Cross off dates that do not apply this month				

KEY: ▮ HEAVY ◥ MEDIUM ◩ LIGHT ● SPOTTING ⊠ N/A

_____ DAYS SINCE LAST PERIOD ♥ EXPECT NEXT PERIOD AROUND _____

Day 1 of Cycle

CRAVINGS ☐   BACKACHE ☐   ENERGY ☺ ☺ ☹
ACNE ☐   HEADACHE ☐   MOOD ☺ ☺ ☹
CRAMPS ☐   SORE BREASTS ☐   SLEEP ☺ ☺ ☹

....
....
....

Day 2 of Cycle

CRAVINGS ☐   BACKACHE ☐   ENERGY ☺ ☺ ☹
ACNE ☐   HEADACHE ☐   MOOD ☺ ☺ ☹
CRAMPS ☐   SORE BREASTS ☐   SLEEP ☺ ☺ ☹

....
....
....

Day 3 of Cycle

CRAVINGS ☐   BACKACHE ☐   ENERGY ☺ ☺ ☹
ACNE ☐   HEADACHE ☐   MOOD ☺ ☺ ☹
CRAMPS ☐   SORE BREASTS ☐   SLEEP ☺ ☺ ☹

....
....
....

Day 4 of Cycle

CRAVINGS ☐ BACKACHE ☐ ENERGY 😀 😐 😞
ACNE ☐ HEADACHE ☐ MOOD 😀 😐 😞
CRAMPS ☐ SORE BREASTS ☐ SLEEP 😀 😐 😞

....
....
....

Day 5 of Cycle

CRAVINGS ☐ BACKACHE ☐ ENERGY 😀 😐 😞
ACNE ☐ HEADACHE ☐ MOOD 😀 😐 😞
CRAMPS ☐ SORE BREASTS ☐ SLEEP 😀 😐 😞

....
....
....

Day 6 of Cycle

CRAVINGS ☐ BACKACHE ☐ ENERGY 😀 😐 😞
ACNE ☐ HEADACHE ☐ MOOD 😀 😐 😞
CRAMPS ☐ SORE BREASTS ☐ SLEEP 😀 😐 😞

....
....
....

Day 7 of Cycle

CRAVINGS ☐ BACKACHE ☐ ENERGY 😀 😐 😞
ACNE ☐ HEADACHE ☐ MOOD 😀 😐 😞
CRAMPS ☐ SORE BREASTS ☐ SLEEP 😀 😐 😞

....
....
....

1	2	3	4	5	6	7	8	9	10	11	12
13	14	15	16	17	18	19	20	21	22	23	24
25	26	27	28	29	30	31	*Cross off dates that do not apply this month				

KEY: ■ HEAVY ◢ MEDIUM ◩ LIGHT • SPOTTING ⊠ N/A

_____ DAYS SINCE LAST PERIOD ♥ EXPECT NEXT PERIOD AROUND _____

Day 1 of Cycle

CRAVINGS ☐   BACKACHE ☐   ENERGY 😊 😐 ☹
ACNE ☐   HEADACHE ☐   MOOD 😊 😐 ☹
CRAMPS ☐   SORE BREASTS ☐   SLEEP 😊 😐 ☹

....
....
....

Day 2 of Cycle

CRAVINGS ☐   BACKACHE ☐   ENERGY 😊 😐 ☹
ACNE ☐   HEADACHE ☐   MOOD 😊 😐 ☹
CRAMPS ☐   SORE BREASTS ☐   SLEEP 😊 😐 ☹

....
....
....

Day 3 of Cycle

CRAVINGS ☐   BACKACHE ☐   ENERGY 😊 😐 ☹
ACNE ☐   HEADACHE ☐   MOOD 😊 😐 ☹
CRAMPS ☐   SORE BREASTS ☐   SLEEP 😊 😐 ☹

....
....
....

Day 4 of Cycle

CRAVINGS ☐   BACKACHE ☐   ENERGY ☺ ☺ ☹
ACNE ☐   HEADACHE ☐   MOOD ☺ ☺ ☹
CRAMPS ☐   SORE BREASTS ☐   SLEEP ☺ ☺ ☹

....
....
....

Day 5 of Cycle

CRAVINGS ☐   BACKACHE ☐   ENERGY ☺ ☺ ☹
ACNE ☐   HEADACHE ☐   MOOD ☺ ☺ ☹
CRAMPS ☐   SORE BREASTS ☐   SLEEP ☺ ☺ ☹

....
....
....

Day 6 of Cycle

CRAVINGS ☐   BACKACHE ☐   ENERGY ☺ ☺ ☹
ACNE ☐   HEADACHE ☐   MOOD ☺ ☺ ☹
CRAMPS ☐   SORE BREASTS ☐   SLEEP ☺ ☺ ☹

....
....
....

Day 7 of Cycle

CRAVINGS ☐   BACKACHE ☐   ENERGY ☺ ☺ ☹
ACNE ☐   HEADACHE ☐   MOOD ☺ ☺ ☹
CRAMPS ☐   SORE BREASTS ☐   SLEEP ☺ ☺ ☹

....
....
....

| J | F | M | A | M | J | J | A | S | O | N | D |

1	2	3	4	5	6	7	8	9	10	11	12
13	14	15	16	17	18	19	20	21	22	23	24
25	26	27	28	29	30	31	*Cross off dates that do not apply this month				

KEY: ■ HEAVY ◤ MEDIUM ◩ LIGHT • SPOTTING ⊠ N/A

_____ DAYS SINCE LAST PERIOD ♥ EXPECT NEXT PERIOD AROUND _____

Day 1 of Cycle

CRAVINGS ☐   BACKACHE ☐   ENERGY ☺ ☺ ☹
ACNE ☐   HEADACHE ☐   MOOD ☺ ☺ ☹
CRAMPS ☐   SORE BREASTS ☐   SLEEP ☺ ☺ ☹

....
....
....

Day 2 of Cycle

CRAVINGS ☐   BACKACHE ☐   ENERGY ☺ ☺ ☹
ACNE ☐   HEADACHE ☐   MOOD ☺ ☺ ☹
CRAMPS ☐   SORE BREASTS ☐   SLEEP ☺ ☺ ☹

....
....
....

Day 3 of Cycle

CRAVINGS ☐   BACKACHE ☐   ENERGY ☺ ☺ ☹
ACNE ☐   HEADACHE ☐   MOOD ☺ ☺ ☹
CRAMPS ☐   SORE BREASTS ☐   SLEEP ☺ ☺ ☹

....
....
....

Day 4 of Cycle

CRAVINGS ☐   BACKACHE ☐   ENERGY 😄 😐 😞
ACNE ☐   HEADACHE ☐   MOOD 😄 😐 😞
CRAMPS ☐   SORE BREASTS ☐   SLEEP 😄 😐 😞

....
....
....

Day 5 of Cycle

CRAVINGS ☐   BACKACHE ☐   ENERGY 😄 😐 😞
ACNE ☐   HEADACHE ☐   MOOD 😄 😐 😞
CRAMPS ☐   SORE BREASTS ☐   SLEEP 😄 😐 😞

....
....
....

Day 6 of Cycle

CRAVINGS ☐   BACKACHE ☐   ENERGY 😄 😐 😞
ACNE ☐   HEADACHE ☐   MOOD 😄 😐 😞
CRAMPS ☐   SORE BREASTS ☐   SLEEP 😄 😐 😞

....
....
....

Day 7 of Cycle

CRAVINGS ☐   BACKACHE ☐   ENERGY 😄 😐 😞
ACNE ☐   HEADACHE ☐   MOOD 😄 😐 😞
CRAMPS ☐   SORE BREASTS ☐   SLEEP 😄 😐 😞

....
....
....

| J | F | m | A | m | J | J | A | S | O | N | D |

1	2	3	4	5	6	7	8	9	10	11	12
13	14	15	16	17	18	19	20	21	22	23	24
25	26	27	28	29	30	31	*Cross off dates that do not apply this month				

KEY: ■ HEAVY ◢ MEDIUM ▧ LIGHT • SPOTTING ⊠ N/A

_____ DAYS SINCE LAST PERIOD ♥ EXPECT NEXT PERIOD AROUND _____

Day 1 of Cycle

CRAVINGS ☐   BACKACHE ☐   ENERGY 😀 😐 🙁
ACNE ☐   HEADACHE ☐   MOOD 😀 😐 🙁
CRAMPS ☐   SORE BREASTS ☐   SLEEP 😀 😐 🙁

....
....
....

Day 2 of Cycle

CRAVINGS ☐   BACKACHE ☐   ENERGY 😀 😐 🙁
ACNE ☐   HEADACHE ☐   MOOD 😀 😐 🙁
CRAMPS ☐   SORE BREASTS ☐   SLEEP 😀 😐 🙁

....
....
....

Day 3 of Cycle

CRAVINGS ☐   BACKACHE ☐   ENERGY 😀 😐 🙁
ACNE ☐   HEADACHE ☐   MOOD 😀 😐 🙁
CRAMPS ☐   SORE BREASTS ☐   SLEEP 😀 😐 🙁

....
....
....

Day 4 of Cycle

CRAVINGS ☐   BACKACHE ☐   ENERGY 🙂 😐 🙁
ACNE ☐   HEADACHE ☐   MOOD 🙂 😐 🙁
CRAMPS ☐   SORE BREASTS ☐   SLEEP 🙂 😐 🙁

....
....
....

Day 5 of Cycle

CRAVINGS ☐   BACKACHE ☐   ENERGY 🙂 😐 🙁
ACNE ☐   HEADACHE ☐   MOOD 🙂 😐 🙁
CRAMPS ☐   SORE BREASTS ☐   SLEEP 🙂 😐 🙁

....
....
....

Day 6 of Cycle

CRAVINGS ☐   BACKACHE ☐   ENERGY 🙂 😐 🙁
ACNE ☐   HEADACHE ☐   MOOD 🙂 😐 🙁
CRAMPS ☐   SORE BREASTS ☐   SLEEP 🙂 😐 🙁

....
....
....

Day 7 of Cycle

CRAVINGS ☐   BACKACHE ☐   ENERGY 🙂 😐 🙁
ACNE ☐   HEADACHE ☐   MOOD 🙂 😐 🙁
CRAMPS ☐   SORE BREASTS ☐   SLEEP 🙂 😐 🙁

....
....
....

J	F	M	A	M	J	J	A	S	O	N	D

1	2	3	4	5	6	7	8	9	10	11	12
13	14	15	16	17	18	19	20	21	22	23	24
25	26	27	28	29	30	31	*Cross off dates that do not apply this month				

KEY: ■ HEAVY ◪ MEDIUM ◨ LIGHT • SPOTTING ⊠ N/A

_____ DAYS SINCE LAST PERIOD ♥ EXPECT NEXT PERIOD AROUND _____

Day 1 of Cycle

CRAVINGS ☐   BACKACHE ☐   ENERGY 🙂 😐 🙁
ACNE ☐   HEADACHE ☐   MOOD 🙂 😐 🙁
CRAMPS ☐   SORE BREASTS ☐   SLEEP 🙂 😐 🙁

....
....
....

Day 2 of Cycle

CRAVINGS ☐   BACKACHE ☐   ENERGY 🙂 😐 🙁
ACNE ☐   HEADACHE ☐   MOOD 🙂 😐 🙁
CRAMPS ☐   SORE BREASTS ☐   SLEEP 🙂 😐 🙁

....
....
....

Day 3 of Cycle

CRAVINGS ☐   BACKACHE ☐   ENERGY 🙂 😐 🙁
ACNE ☐   HEADACHE ☐   MOOD 🙂 😐 🙁
CRAMPS ☐   SORE BREASTS ☐   SLEEP 🙂 😐 🙁

....
....
....

Day 4 of Cycle

CRAVINGS ☐   BACKACHE ☐   ENERGY 😊 😐 ☹
ACNE ☐   HEADACHE ☐   MOOD 😊 😐 ☹
CRAMPS ☐   SORE BREASTS ☐   SLEEP 😊 😐 ☹

....
....
....

Day 5 of Cycle

CRAVINGS ☐   BACKACHE ☐   ENERGY 😊 😐 ☹
ACNE ☐   HEADACHE ☐   MOOD 😊 😐 ☹
CRAMPS ☐   SORE BREASTS ☐   SLEEP 😊 😐 ☹

....
....
....

Day 6 of Cycle

CRAVINGS ☐   BACKACHE ☐   ENERGY 😊 😐 ☹
ACNE ☐   HEADACHE ☐   MOOD 😊 😐 ☹
CRAMPS ☐   SORE BREASTS ☐   SLEEP 😊 😐 ☹

....
....
....

Day 7 of Cycle

CRAVINGS ☐   BACKACHE ☐   ENERGY 😊 😐 ☹
ACNE ☐   HEADACHE ☐   MOOD 😊 😐 ☹
CRAMPS ☐   SORE BREASTS ☐   SLEEP 😊 😐 ☹

....
....
....

J	F	m	A	m	J	J	A	S	O	N	D

1	2	3	4	5	6	7	8	9	10	11	12
13	14	15	16	17	18	19	20	21	22	23	24
25	26	27	28	29	30	31	*Cross off dates that do not apply this month				

KEY: ■ HEAVY ◢ MEDIUM ▧ LIGHT ● SPOTTING ⊠ N/A

_____ DAYS SINCE LAST PERIOD ♥ EXPECT NEXT PERIOD AROUND _____

Day 1 of Cycle

CRAVINGS ☐　　　BACKACHE ☐　　　ENERGY 😀 😐 🙁
ACNE ☐　　　HEADACHE ☐　　　MOOD 😀 😐 🙁
CRAMPS ☐　　　SORE BREASTS ☐　　　SLEEP 😀 😐 🙁

....
....
....

Day 2 of Cycle

CRAVINGS ☐　　　BACKACHE ☐　　　ENERGY 😀 😐 🙁
ACNE ☐　　　HEADACHE ☐　　　MOOD 😀 😐 🙁
CRAMPS ☐　　　SORE BREASTS ☐　　　SLEEP 😀 😐 🙁

....
....
....

Day 3 of Cycle

CRAVINGS ☐　　　BACKACHE ☐　　　ENERGY 😀 😐 🙁
ACNE ☐　　　HEADACHE ☐　　　MOOD 😀 😐 🙁
CRAMPS ☐　　　SORE BREASTS ☐　　　SLEEP 😀 😐 🙁

....
....
....

YEAR:_____

Day 4 of Cycle

CRAVINGS ☐   BACKACHE ☐   ENERGY 😊 😐 ☹️
ACNE ☐   HEADACHE ☐   MOOD 😊 😐 ☹️
CRAMPS ☐   SORE BREASTS ☐   SLEEP 😊 😐 ☹️

....
....
....

Day 5 of Cycle

CRAVINGS ☐   BACKACHE ☐   ENERGY 😊 😐 ☹️
ACNE ☐   HEADACHE ☐   MOOD 😊 😐 ☹️
CRAMPS ☐   SORE BREASTS ☐   SLEEP 😊 😐 ☹️

....
....
....

Day 6 of Cycle

CRAVINGS ☐   BACKACHE ☐   ENERGY 😊 😐 ☹️
ACNE ☐   HEADACHE ☐   MOOD 😊 😐 ☹️
CRAMPS ☐   SORE BREASTS ☐   SLEEP 😊 😐 ☹️

....
....
....

Day 7 of Cycle

CRAVINGS ☐   BACKACHE ☐   ENERGY 😊 😐 ☹️
ACNE ☐   HEADACHE ☐   MOOD 😊 😐 ☹️
CRAMPS ☐   SORE BREASTS ☐   SLEEP 😊 😐 ☹️

....
....
....

J	F	M	A	M	J	J	A	S	O	N	D

1	2	3	4	5	6	7	8	9	10	11	12
13	14	15	16	17	18	19	20	21	22	23	24
25	26	27	28	29	30	31	*Cross off dates that do not apply this month

KEY: ■ HEAVY ◪ MEDIUM ⧅ LIGHT ⊡ SPOTTING ⊠ N/A

_____ DAYS SINCE LAST PERIOD ♥ EXPECT NEXT PERIOD AROUND _____

Day 1 of Cycle

CRAVINGS ☐   BACKACHE ☐   ENERGY ☺ 😐 ☹
ACNE ☐   HEADACHE ☐   MOOD ☺ 😐 ☹
CRAMPS ☐   SORE BREASTS ☐   SLEEP ☺ 😐 ☹

....
....
....

Day 2 of Cycle

CRAVINGS ☐   BACKACHE ☐   ENERGY ☺ 😐 ☹
ACNE ☐   HEADACHE ☐   MOOD ☺ 😐 ☹
CRAMPS ☐   SORE BREASTS ☐   SLEEP ☺ 😐 ☹

....
....
....

Day 3 of Cycle

CRAVINGS ☐   BACKACHE ☐   ENERGY ☺ 😐 ☹
ACNE ☐   HEADACHE ☐   MOOD ☺ 😐 ☹
CRAMPS ☐   SORE BREASTS ☐   SLEEP ☺ 😐 ☹

....
....
....

YEAR:_____

Day 4 of Cycle

CRAVINGS ☐   BACKACHE ☐   ENERGY 😊 😐 😞
ACNE ☐   HEADACHE ☐   MOOD 😊 😐 😞
CRAMPS ☐   SORE BREASTS ☐   SLEEP 😊 😐 😞

....
....
....

Day 5 of Cycle

CRAVINGS ☐   BACKACHE ☐   ENERGY 😊 😐 😞
ACNE ☐   HEADACHE ☐   MOOD 😊 😐 😞
CRAMPS ☐   SORE BREASTS ☐   SLEEP 😊 😐 😞

....
....
....

Day 6 of Cycle

CRAVINGS ☐   BACKACHE ☐   ENERGY 😊 😐 😞
ACNE ☐   HEADACHE ☐   MOOD 😊 😐 😞
CRAMPS ☐   SORE BREASTS ☐   SLEEP 😊 😐 😞

....
....
....

Day 7 of Cycle

CRAVINGS ☐   BACKACHE ☐   ENERGY 😊 😐 😞
ACNE ☐   HEADACHE ☐   MOOD 😊 😐 😞
CRAMPS ☐   SORE BREASTS ☐   SLEEP 😊 😐 😞

....
....
....

J	F	M	A	M	J	J	A	S	O	N	D

1	2	3	4	5	6	7	8	9	10	11	12
13	14	15	16	17	18	19	20	21	22	23	24
25	26	27	28	29	30	31	*Cross off dates that do not apply this month				

KEY: ■ HEAVY ◤ MEDIUM ▧ LIGHT ▣ SPOTTING ⊠ N/A

_____ DAYS SINCE LAST PERIOD ♥ EXPECT NEXT PERIOD AROUND _____

Day 1 of Cycle

CRAVINGS ☐   BACKACHE ☐   ENERGY ☺ 😐 ☹
ACNE ☐   HEADACHE ☐   MOOD ☺ 😐 ☹
CRAMPS ☐   SORE BREASTS ☐   SLEEP ☺ 😐 ☹

....
....
....

Day 2 of Cycle

CRAVINGS ☐   BACKACHE ☐   ENERGY ☺ 😐 ☹
ACNE ☐   HEADACHE ☐   MOOD ☺ 😐 ☹
CRAMPS ☐   SORE BREASTS ☐   SLEEP ☺ 😐 ☹

....
....
....

Day 3 of Cycle

CRAVINGS ☐   BACKACHE ☐   ENERGY ☺ 😐 ☹
ACNE ☐   HEADACHE ☐   MOOD ☺ 😐 ☹
CRAMPS ☐   SORE BREASTS ☐   SLEEP ☺ 😐 ☹

....
....
....

Day 4 of Cycle

CRAVINGS ☐   BACKACHE ☐   ENERGY 😃 😐 ☹️
ACNE ☐   HEADACHE ☐   MOOD 😃 😐 ☹️
CRAMPS ☐   SORE BREASTS ☐   SLEEP 😃 😐 ☹️

....
....
....

Day 5 of Cycle

CRAVINGS ☐   BACKACHE ☐   ENERGY 😃 😐 ☹️
ACNE ☐   HEADACHE ☐   MOOD 😃 😐 ☹️
CRAMPS ☐   SORE BREASTS ☐   SLEEP 😃 😐 ☹️

....
....
....

Day 6 of Cycle

CRAVINGS ☐   BACKACHE ☐   ENERGY 😃 😐 ☹️
ACNE ☐   HEADACHE ☐   MOOD 😃 😐 ☹️
CRAMPS ☐   SORE BREASTS ☐   SLEEP 😃 😐 ☹️

....
....
....

Day 7 of Cycle

CRAVINGS ☐   BACKACHE ☐   ENERGY 😃 😐 ☹️
ACNE ☐   HEADACHE ☐   MOOD 😃 😐 ☹️
CRAMPS ☐   SORE BREASTS ☐   SLEEP 😃 😐 ☹️

....
....
....

(J)	(F)	(m)	(A)	(m)	(J)	(J)	(A)	(S)	(O)	(N)	(D)

1	2	3	4	5	6	7	8	9	10	11	12
13	14	15	16	17	18	19	20	21	22	23	24
25	26	27	28	29	30	31	*Cross off dates that do not apply this month				

KEY: ■ HEAVY ◣ MEDIUM ◩ LIGHT ⊙ SPOTTING ⊠ N/A

_____ DAYS SINCE LAST PERIOD ♥ EXPECT NEXT PERIOD AROUND _____

Day 1 of Cycle

CRAVINGS ☐   BACKACHE ☐   ENERGY ☺ ☺ ☹
ACNE ☐   HEADACHE ☐   MOOD ☺ ☺ ☹
CRAMPS ☐   SORE BREASTS ☐   SLEEP ☺ ☺ ☹

....
....
....

Day 2 of Cycle

CRAVINGS ☐   BACKACHE ☐   ENERGY ☺ ☺ ☹
ACNE ☐   HEADACHE ☐   MOOD ☺ ☺ ☹
CRAMPS ☐   SORE BREASTS ☐   SLEEP ☺ ☺ ☹

....
....
....

Day 3 of Cycle

CRAVINGS ☐   BACKACHE ☐   ENERGY ☺ ☺ ☹
ACNE ☐   HEADACHE ☐   MOOD ☺ ☺ ☹
CRAMPS ☐   SORE BREASTS ☐   SLEEP ☺ ☺ ☹

....
....
....

Day 4 of Cycle

CRAVINGS ☐   BACKACHE ☐   ENERGY 😀 😐 🙁
ACNE ☐   HEADACHE ☐   MOOD 😀 😐 🙁
CRAMPS ☐   SORE BREASTS ☐   SLEEP 😀 😐 🙁

....
....
....

Day 5 of Cycle

CRAVINGS ☐   BACKACHE ☐   ENERGY 😀 😐 🙁
ACNE ☐   HEADACHE ☐   MOOD 😀 😐 🙁
CRAMPS ☐   SORE BREASTS ☐   SLEEP 😀 😐 🙁

....
....
....

Day 6 of Cycle

CRAVINGS ☐   BACKACHE ☐   ENERGY 😀 😐 🙁
ACNE ☐   HEADACHE ☐   MOOD 😀 😐 🙁
CRAMPS ☐   SORE BREASTS ☐   SLEEP 😀 😐 🙁

....
....
....

Day 7 of Cycle

CRAVINGS ☐   BACKACHE ☐   ENERGY 😀 😐 🙁
ACNE ☐   HEADACHE ☐   MOOD 😀 😐 🙁
CRAMPS ☐   SORE BREASTS ☐   SLEEP 😀 😐 🙁

....
....
....

J	F	m	A	m	J	J	A	S	O	N	D

1	2	3	4	5	6	7	8	9	10	11	12
13	14	15	16	17	18	19	20	21	22	23	24
25	26	27	28	29	30	31	*Cross off dates that do not apply this month				

KEY: ■ HEAVY ◪ MEDIUM ◩ LIGHT • SPOTTING ⊠ N/A

_____ DAYS SINCE LAST PERIOD ♥ EXPECT NEXT PERIOD AROUND _____

Day 1 of Cycle

CRAVINGS ☐   BACKACHE ☐   ENERGY 😊 😐 ☹
ACNE ☐   HEADACHE ☐   MOOD 😊 😐 ☹
CRAMPS ☐   SORE BREASTS ☐   SLEEP 😊 😐 ☹

....
....
....

Day 2 of Cycle

CRAVINGS ☐   BACKACHE ☐   ENERGY 😊 😐 ☹
ACNE ☐   HEADACHE ☐   MOOD 😊 😐 ☹
CRAMPS ☐   SORE BREASTS ☐   SLEEP 😊 😐 ☹

....
....
....

Day 3 of Cycle

CRAVINGS ☐   BACKACHE ☐   ENERGY 😊 😐 ☹
ACNE ☐   HEADACHE ☐   MOOD 😊 😐 ☹
CRAMPS ☐   SORE BREASTS ☐   SLEEP 😊 😐 ☹

....
....
....

Day 4 of Cycle

CRAVINGS ☐   BACKACHE ☐   ENERGY 😀 😐 ☹️
ACNE ☐   HEADACHE ☐   MOOD 😀 😐 ☹️
CRAMPS ☐   SORE BREASTS ☐   SLEEP 😀 😐 ☹️

....
....
....

Day 5 of Cycle

CRAVINGS ☐   BACKACHE ☐   ENERGY 😀 😐 ☹️
ACNE ☐   HEADACHE ☐   MOOD 😀 😐 ☹️
CRAMPS ☐   SORE BREASTS ☐   SLEEP 😀 😐 ☹️

....
....
....

Day 6 of Cycle

CRAVINGS ☐   BACKACHE ☐   ENERGY 😀 😐 ☹️
ACNE ☐   HEADACHE ☐   MOOD 😀 😐 ☹️
CRAMPS ☐   SORE BREASTS ☐   SLEEP 😀 😐 ☹️

....
....
....

Day 7 of Cycle

CRAVINGS ☐   BACKACHE ☐   ENERGY 😀 😐 ☹️
ACNE ☐   HEADACHE ☐   MOOD 😀 😐 ☹️
CRAMPS ☐   SORE BREASTS ☐   SLEEP 😀 😐 ☹️

....
....
....

J	F	(m)	(A)	(m)	J	J	(A)	(S)	(O)	(N)	(D)

1	2	3	4	5	6	7	8	9	10	11	12
13	14	15	16	17	18	19	20	21	22	23	24
25	26	27	28	29	30	31	*Cross off dates that do not apply this month

KEY: ■ HEAVY ◣ MEDIUM ◨ LIGHT ● SPOTTING ⊠ N/A

_____ DAYS SINCE LAST PERIOD ♥ EXPECT NEXT PERIOD AROUND _____

Day 1 of Cycle

CRAVINGS ☐   BACKACHE ☐   ENERGY ☺ 😐 ☹
ACNE ☐   HEADACHE ☐   MOOD ☺ 😐 ☹
CRAMPS ☐   SORE BREASTS ☐   SLEEP ☺ 😐 ☹

....
....
....

Day 2 of Cycle

CRAVINGS ☐   BACKACHE ☐   ENERGY ☺ 😐 ☹
ACNE ☐   HEADACHE ☐   MOOD ☺ 😐 ☹
CRAMPS ☐   SORE BREASTS ☐   SLEEP ☺ 😐 ☹

....
....
....

Day 3 of Cycle

CRAVINGS ☐   BACKACHE ☐   ENERGY ☺ 😐 ☹
ACNE ☐   HEADACHE ☐   MOOD ☺ 😐 ☹
CRAMPS ☐   SORE BREASTS ☐   SLEEP ☺ 😐 ☹

....
....
....

YEAR:_____

Day 4 of Cycle

CRAVINGS ☐   BACKACHE ☐   ENERGY 😊 😐 ☹
ACNE ☐   HEADACHE ☐   MOOD 😊 😐 ☹
CRAMPS ☐   SORE BREASTS ☐   SLEEP 😊 😐 ☹

....
....
....

Day 5 of Cycle

CRAVINGS ☐   BACKACHE ☐   ENERGY 😊 😐 ☹
ACNE ☐   HEADACHE ☐   MOOD 😊 😐 ☹
CRAMPS ☐   SORE BREASTS ☐   SLEEP 😊 😐 ☹

....
....
....

Day 6 of Cycle

CRAVINGS ☐   BACKACHE ☐   ENERGY 😊 😐 ☹
ACNE ☐   HEADACHE ☐   MOOD 😊 😐 ☹
CRAMPS ☐   SORE BREASTS ☐   SLEEP 😊 😐 ☹

....
....
....

Day 7 of Cycle

CRAVINGS ☐   BACKACHE ☐   ENERGY 😊 😐 ☹
ACNE ☐   HEADACHE ☐   MOOD 😊 😐 ☹
CRAMPS ☐   SORE BREASTS ☐   SLEEP 😊 😐 ☹

....
....
....

J	F	m	A	m	J	J	A	S	O	N	D

1	2	3	4	5	6	7	8	9	10	11	12
13	14	15	16	17	18	19	20	21	22	23	24
25	26	27	28	29	30	31	*Cross off dates that do not apply this month				

KEY: ■ HEAVY ◤ MEDIUM ◩ LIGHT ⊡ SPOTTING ⊠ N/A

_____ DAYS SINCE LAST PERIOD ♥ EXPECT NEXT PERIOD AROUND _____

Day 1 of Cycle

CRAVINGS ☐   BACKACHE ☐   ENERGY ☺ 😐 ☹
ACNE ☐   HEADACHE ☐   MOOD ☺ 😐 ☹
CRAMPS ☐   SORE BREASTS ☐   SLEEP ☺ 😐 ☹

....
....
....

Day 2 of Cycle

CRAVINGS ☐   BACKACHE ☐   ENERGY ☺ 😐 ☹
ACNE ☐   HEADACHE ☐   MOOD ☺ 😐 ☹
CRAMPS ☐   SORE BREASTS ☐   SLEEP ☺ 😐 ☹

....
....
....

Day 3 of Cycle

CRAVINGS ☐   BACKACHE ☐   ENERGY ☺ 😐 ☹
ACNE ☐   HEADACHE ☐   MOOD ☺ 😐 ☹
CRAMPS ☐   SORE BREASTS ☐   SLEEP ☺ 😐 ☹

....
....
....

YEAR:_____

Day 4 of Cycle

CRAVINGS ☐   BACKACHE ☐   ENERGY 😀 😐 🙁
ACNE ☐   HEADACHE ☐   MOOD 😀 😐 🙁
CRAMPS ☐   SORE BREASTS ☐   SLEEP 😀 😐 🙁

....
....
....

Day 5 of Cycle

CRAVINGS ☐   BACKACHE ☐   ENERGY 😀 😐 🙁
ACNE ☐   HEADACHE ☐   MOOD 😀 😐 🙁
CRAMPS ☐   SORE BREASTS ☐   SLEEP 😀 😐 🙁

....
....
....

Day 6 of Cycle

CRAVINGS ☐   BACKACHE ☐   ENERGY 😀 😐 🙁
ACNE ☐   HEADACHE ☐   MOOD 😀 😐 🙁
CRAMPS ☐   SORE BREASTS ☐   SLEEP 😀 😐 🙁

....
....
....

Day 7 of Cycle

CRAVINGS ☐   BACKACHE ☐   ENERGY 😀 😐 🙁
ACNE ☐   HEADACHE ☐   MOOD 😀 😐 🙁
CRAMPS ☐   SORE BREASTS ☐   SLEEP 😀 😐 🙁

....
....
....

J	F	M	A	M	J	J	A	S	O	N	D

1	2	3	4	5	6	7	8	9	10	11	12
13	14	15	16	17	18	19	20	21	22	23	24
25	26	27	28	29	30	31	*Cross off dates that do not apply this month				

KEY: ▨ HEAVY ◣ MEDIUM ◩ LIGHT ● SPOTTING ⊠ N/A

_____ DAYS SINCE LAST PERIOD 💜 EXPECT NEXT PERIOD AROUND _____

Day 1 of Cycle

CRAVINGS ☐   BACKACHE ☐   ENERGY 🙂 😐 🙁
ACNE ☐   HEADACHE ☐   MOOD 🙂 😐 🙁
CRAMPS ☐   SORE BREASTS ☐   SLEEP 🙂 😐 🙁

....
....
....

Day 2 of Cycle

CRAVINGS ☐   BACKACHE ☐   ENERGY 🙂 😐 🙁
ACNE ☐   HEADACHE ☐   MOOD 🙂 😐 🙁
CRAMPS ☐   SORE BREASTS ☐   SLEEP 🙂 😐 🙁

....
....
....

Day 3 of Cycle

CRAVINGS ☐   BACKACHE ☐   ENERGY 🙂 😐 🙁
ACNE ☐   HEADACHE ☐   MOOD 🙂 😐 🙁
CRAMPS ☐   SORE BREASTS ☐   SLEEP 🙂 😐 🙁

....
....
....

Day 4 of Cycle

CRAVINGS ☐   BACKACHE ☐   ENERGY 😊 😐 ☹
ACNE ☐   HEADACHE ☐   MOOD 😊 😐 ☹
CRAMPS ☐   SORE BREASTS ☐   SLEEP 😊 😐 ☹

....
....
....

Day 5 of Cycle

CRAVINGS ☐   BACKACHE ☐   ENERGY 😊 😐 ☹
ACNE ☐   HEADACHE ☐   MOOD 😊 😐 ☹
CRAMPS ☐   SORE BREASTS ☐   SLEEP 😊 😐 ☹

....
....
....

Day 6 of Cycle

CRAVINGS ☐   BACKACHE ☐   ENERGY 😊 😐 ☹
ACNE ☐   HEADACHE ☐   MOOD 😊 😐 ☹
CRAMPS ☐   SORE BREASTS ☐   SLEEP 😊 😐 ☹

....
....
....

Day 7 of Cycle

CRAVINGS ☐   BACKACHE ☐   ENERGY 😊 😐 ☹
ACNE ☐   HEADACHE ☐   MOOD 😊 😐 ☹
CRAMPS ☐   SORE BREASTS ☐   SLEEP 😊 😐 ☹

....
....
....

| J | F | M | A | M | J | J | A | S | O | N | D |

1	2	3	4	5	6	7	8	9	10	11	12
13	14	15	16	17	18	19	20	21	22	23	24
25	26	27	28	29	30	31	*Cross off dates that do not apply this month				

KEY: ■ HEAVY ◢ MEDIUM ◩ LIGHT • SPOTTING ⊠ N/A

_____ DAYS SINCE LAST PERIOD 🖤 EXPECT NEXT PERIOD AROUND _____

Day 1 of Cycle

CRAVINGS ☐   BACKACHE ☐   ENERGY 😊 😐 😟
ACNE ☐   HEADACHE ☐   MOOD 😊 😐 😟
CRAMPS ☐   SORE BREASTS ☐   SLEEP 😊 😐 😟

....
....
....

Day 2 of Cycle

CRAVINGS ☐   BACKACHE ☐   ENERGY 😊 😐 😟
ACNE ☐   HEADACHE ☐   MOOD 😊 😐 😟
CRAMPS ☐   SORE BREASTS ☐   SLEEP 😊 😐 😟

....
....
....

Day 3 of Cycle

CRAVINGS ☐   BACKACHE ☐   ENERGY 😊 😐 😟
ACNE ☐   HEADACHE ☐   MOOD 😊 😐 😟
CRAMPS ☐   SORE BREASTS ☐   SLEEP 😊 😐 😟

....
....
....

Day 4 of Cycle

CRAVINGS ☐   BACKACHE ☐   ENERGY 😃 😐 ☹
ACNE ☐   HEADACHE ☐   MOOD 😃 😐 ☹
CRAMPS ☐   SORE BREASTS ☐   SLEEP 😃 😐 ☹

....
....
....

Day 5 of Cycle

CRAVINGS ☐   BACKACHE ☐   ENERGY 😃 😐 ☹
ACNE ☐   HEADACHE ☐   MOOD 😃 😐 ☹
CRAMPS ☐   SORE BREASTS ☐   SLEEP 😃 😐 ☹

....
....
....

Day 6 of Cycle

CRAVINGS ☐   BACKACHE ☐   ENERGY 😃 😐 ☹
ACNE ☐   HEADACHE ☐   MOOD 😃 😐 ☹
CRAMPS ☐   SORE BREASTS ☐   SLEEP 😃 😐 ☹

....
....
....

Day 7 of Cycle

CRAVINGS ☐   BACKACHE ☐   ENERGY 😃 😐 ☹
ACNE ☐   HEADACHE ☐   MOOD 😃 😐 ☹
CRAMPS ☐   SORE BREASTS ☐   SLEEP 😃 😐 ☹

....
....
....

| J | F | M | A | M | J | J | A | S | O | N | D |

1	2	3	4	5	6	7	8	9	10	11	12
13	14	15	16	17	18	19	20	21	22	23	24
25	26	27	28	29	30	31	*Cross off dates that do not apply this month

KEY: ■ HEAVY ◢ MEDIUM ◨ LIGHT ● SPOTTING ⊠ N/A

_____ DAYS SINCE LAST PERIOD ♥ EXPECT NEXT PERIOD AROUND _____

Day 1 of Cycle

CRAVINGS ☐   BACKACHE ☐   ENERGY 😊 😐 ☹
ACNE ☐   HEADACHE ☐   MOOD 😊 😐 ☹
CRAMPS ☐   SORE BREASTS ☐   SLEEP 😊 😐 ☹

....
....
....

Day 2 of Cycle

CRAVINGS ☐   BACKACHE ☐   ENERGY 😊 😐 ☹
ACNE ☐   HEADACHE ☐   MOOD 😊 😐 ☹
CRAMPS ☐   SORE BREASTS ☐   SLEEP 😊 😐 ☹

....
....
....

Day 3 of Cycle

CRAVINGS ☐   BACKACHE ☐   ENERGY 😊 😐 ☹
ACNE ☐   HEADACHE ☐   MOOD 😊 😐 ☹
CRAMPS ☐   SORE BREASTS ☐   SLEEP 😊 😐 ☹

....
....
....

Day 4 of Cycle

CRAVINGS ☐   BACKACHE ☐   ENERGY 😊 😐 ☹️
ACNE ☐   HEADACHE ☐   MOOD 😊 😐 ☹️
CRAMPS ☐   SORE BREASTS ☐   SLEEP 😊 😐 ☹️

....
....
....

Day 5 of Cycle

CRAVINGS ☐   BACKACHE ☐   ENERGY 😊 😐 ☹️
ACNE ☐   HEADACHE ☐   MOOD 😊 😐 ☹️
CRAMPS ☐   SORE BREASTS ☐   SLEEP 😊 😐 ☹️

....
....
....

Day 6 of Cycle

CRAVINGS ☐   BACKACHE ☐   ENERGY 😊 😐 ☹️
ACNE ☐   HEADACHE ☐   MOOD 😊 😐 ☹️
CRAMPS ☐   SORE BREASTS ☐   SLEEP 😊 😐 ☹️

....
....
....

Day 7 of Cycle

CRAVINGS ☐   BACKACHE ☐   ENERGY 😊 😐 ☹️
ACNE ☐   HEADACHE ☐   MOOD 😊 😐 ☹️
CRAMPS ☐   SORE BREASTS ☐   SLEEP 😊 😐 ☹️

....
....
....

J	F	M	A	M	J	J	A	S	O	N	D

1	2	3	4	5	6	7	8	9	10	11	12
13	14	15	16	17	18	19	20	21	22	23	24
25	26	27	28	29	30	31	*Cross off dates that do not apply this month				

KEY: ■ HEAVY ◢ MEDIUM ◩ LIGHT • SPOTTING ⊠ N/A

_____ DAYS SINCE LAST PERIOD ♥ EXPECT NEXT PERIOD AROUND _____

Day 1 of Cycle

CRAVINGS ☐   BACKACHE ☐   ENERGY ☺ 😐 ☹
ACNE ☐   HEADACHE ☐   MOOD ☺ 😐 ☹
CRAMPS ☐   SORE BREASTS ☐   SLEEP ☺ 😐 ☹

....
....
....

Day 2 of Cycle

CRAVINGS ☐   BACKACHE ☐   ENERGY ☺ 😐 ☹
ACNE ☐   HEADACHE ☐   MOOD ☺ 😐 ☹
CRAMPS ☐   SORE BREASTS ☐   SLEEP ☺ 😐 ☹

....
....
....

Day 3 of Cycle

CRAVINGS ☐   BACKACHE ☐   ENERGY ☺ 😐 ☹
ACNE ☐   HEADACHE ☐   MOOD ☺ 😐 ☹
CRAMPS ☐   SORE BREASTS ☐   SLEEP ☺ 😐 ☹

....
....
....

YEAR:_____

Day 4 of Cycle

CRAVINGS ☐   BACKACHE ☐   ENERGY 😃 😐 😟
ACNE ☐   HEADACHE ☐   MOOD 😃 😐 😟
CRAMPS ☐   SORE BREASTS ☐   SLEEP 😃 😐 😟

....
....
....

Day 5 of Cycle

CRAVINGS ☐   BACKACHE ☐   ENERGY 😃 😐 😟
ACNE ☐   HEADACHE ☐   MOOD 😃 😐 😟
CRAMPS ☐   SORE BREASTS ☐   SLEEP 😃 😐 😟

....
....
....

Day 6 of Cycle

CRAVINGS ☐   BACKACHE ☐   ENERGY 😃 😐 😟
ACNE ☐   HEADACHE ☐   MOOD 😃 😐 😟
CRAMPS ☐   SORE BREASTS ☐   SLEEP 😃 😐 😟

....
....
....

Day 7 of Cycle

CRAVINGS ☐   BACKACHE ☐   ENERGY 😃 😐 😟
ACNE ☐   HEADACHE ☐   MOOD 😃 😐 😟
CRAMPS ☐   SORE BREASTS ☐   SLEEP 😃 😐 😟

....
....
....

| J | F | M | A | M | J | J | A | S | O | N | D |

1	2	3	4	5	6	7	8	9	10	11	12
13	14	15	16	17	18	19	20	21	22	23	24
25	26	27	28	29	30	31	*Cross off dates that do not apply this month				

KEY: ■ HEAVY ◤ MEDIUM ▨ LIGHT • SPOTTING ⊠ N/A

_____ DAYS SINCE LAST PERIOD ♥ EXPECT NEXT PERIOD AROUND _____

Day 1 of Cycle

CRAVINGS ☐   BACKACHE ☐   ENERGY 😊 😐 ☹️
ACNE ☐   HEADACHE ☐   MOOD 😊 😐 ☹️
CRAMPS ☐   SORE BREASTS ☐   SLEEP 😊 😐 ☹️

....
....
....

Day 2 of Cycle

CRAVINGS ☐   BACKACHE ☐   ENERGY 😊 😐 ☹️
ACNE ☐   HEADACHE ☐   MOOD 😊 😐 ☹️
CRAMPS ☐   SORE BREASTS ☐   SLEEP 😊 😐 ☹️

....
....
....

Day 3 of Cycle

CRAVINGS ☐   BACKACHE ☐   ENERGY 😊 😐 ☹️
ACNE ☐   HEADACHE ☐   MOOD 😊 😐 ☹️
CRAMPS ☐   SORE BREASTS ☐   SLEEP 😊 😐 ☹️

....
....
....

Day 4 of Cycle

CRAVINGS ☐   BACKACHE ☐   ENERGY 😊 😐 ☹
ACNE ☐   HEADACHE ☐   MOOD 😊 😐 ☹
CRAMPS ☐   SORE BREASTS ☐   SLEEP 😊 😐 ☹

....
....
....

Day 5 of Cycle

CRAVINGS ☐   BACKACHE ☐   ENERGY 😊 😐 ☹
ACNE ☐   HEADACHE ☐   MOOD 😊 😐 ☹
CRAMPS ☐   SORE BREASTS ☐   SLEEP 😊 😐 ☹

....
....
....

Day 6 of Cycle

CRAVINGS ☐   BACKACHE ☐   ENERGY 😊 😐 ☹
ACNE ☐   HEADACHE ☐   MOOD 😊 😐 ☹
CRAMPS ☐   SORE BREASTS ☐   SLEEP 😊 😐 ☹

....
....
....

Day 7 of Cycle

CRAVINGS ☐   BACKACHE ☐   ENERGY 😊 😐 ☹
ACNE ☐   HEADACHE ☐   MOOD 😊 😐 ☹
CRAMPS ☐   SORE BREASTS ☐   SLEEP 😊 😐 ☹

....
....
....

| J | F | M | A | M | J | J | A | S | O | N | D |

1	2	3	4	5	6	7	8	9	10	11	12
13	14	15	16	17	18	19	20	21	22	23	24
25	26	27	28	29	30	31	*Cross off dates that do not apply this month				

KEY: ■ HEAVY ◢ MEDIUM ◨ LIGHT • SPOTTING ⊠ N/A

_____ DAYS SINCE LAST PERIOD ♥ EXPECT NEXT PERIOD AROUND _____

Day 1 of Cycle

CRAVINGS ☐   BACKACHE ☐   ENERGY ☺ 😐 ☹
ACNE ☐   HEADACHE ☐   MOOD ☺ 😐 ☹
CRAMPS ☐   SORE BREASTS ☐   SLEEP ☺ 😐 ☹

....
....
....

Day 2 of Cycle

CRAVINGS ☐   BACKACHE ☐   ENERGY ☺ 😐 ☹
ACNE ☐   HEADACHE ☐   MOOD ☺ 😐 ☹
CRAMPS ☐   SORE BREASTS ☐   SLEEP ☺ 😐 ☹

....
....
....

Day 3 of Cycle

CRAVINGS ☐   BACKACHE ☐   ENERGY ☺ 😐 ☹
ACNE ☐   HEADACHE ☐   MOOD ☺ 😐 ☹
CRAMPS ☐   SORE BREASTS ☐   SLEEP ☺ 😐 ☹

....
....
....

YEAR:_____

Day 4 of Cycle

CRAVINGS ☐   BACKACHE ☐   ENERGY 🙂 😐 🙁
ACNE ☐   HEADACHE ☐   MOOD 🙂 😐 🙁
CRAMPS ☐   SORE BREASTS ☐   SLEEP 🙂 😐 🙁

....
....
....

Day 5 of Cycle

CRAVINGS ☐   BACKACHE ☐   ENERGY 🙂 😐 🙁
ACNE ☐   HEADACHE ☐   MOOD 🙂 😐 🙁
CRAMPS ☐   SORE BREASTS ☐   SLEEP 🙂 😐 🙁

....
....
....

Day 6 of Cycle

CRAVINGS ☐   BACKACHE ☐   ENERGY 🙂 😐 🙁
ACNE ☐   HEADACHE ☐   MOOD 🙂 😐 🙁
CRAMPS ☐   SORE BREASTS ☐   SLEEP 🙂 😐 🙁

....
....
....

Day 7 of Cycle

CRAVINGS ☐   BACKACHE ☐   ENERGY 🙂 😐 🙁
ACNE ☐   HEADACHE ☐   MOOD 🙂 😐 🙁
CRAMPS ☐   SORE BREASTS ☐   SLEEP 🙂 😐 🙁

....
....
....

J	F	M	A	M	J	J	A	S	O	N	D
1	2	3	4	5	6	7	8	9	10	11	12
13	14	15	16	17	18	19	20	21	22	23	24
25	26	27	28	29	30	31	*Cross off dates that do not apply this month				

KEY: ■ HEAVY ◤ MEDIUM ⧅ LIGHT ● SPOTTING ⊠ N/A

_____ DAYS SINCE LAST PERIOD ♥ EXPECT NEXT PERIOD AROUND _____

Day 1 of Cycle

CRAVINGS ☐   BACKACHE ☐   ENERGY 😀 😐 ☹
ACNE ☐   HEADACHE ☐   MOOD 😀 😐 ☹
CRAMPS ☐   SORE BREASTS ☐   SLEEP 😀 😐 ☹

....
....
....

Day 2 of Cycle

CRAVINGS ☐   BACKACHE ☐   ENERGY 😀 😐 ☹
ACNE ☐   HEADACHE ☐   MOOD 😀 😐 ☹
CRAMPS ☐   SORE BREASTS ☐   SLEEP 😀 😐 ☹

....
....
....

Day 3 of Cycle

CRAVINGS ☐   BACKACHE ☐   ENERGY 😀 😐 ☹
ACNE ☐   HEADACHE ☐   MOOD 😀 😐 ☹
CRAMPS ☐   SORE BREASTS ☐   SLEEP 😀 😐 ☹

....
....
....

Day 4 of Cycle

CRAVINGS ☐   BACKACHE ☐   ENERGY 😊 😐 ☹️
ACNE ☐   HEADACHE ☐   MOOD 😊 😐 ☹️
CRAMPS ☐   SORE BREASTS ☐   SLEEP 😊 😐 ☹️

· ·
· ·
· ·

Day 5 of Cycle

CRAVINGS ☐   BACKACHE ☐   ENERGY 😊 😐 ☹️
ACNE ☐   HEADACHE ☐   MOOD 😊 😐 ☹️
CRAMPS ☐   SORE BREASTS ☐   SLEEP 😊 😐 ☹️

· ·
· ·
· ·

Day 6 of Cycle

CRAVINGS ☐   BACKACHE ☐   ENERGY 😊 😐 ☹️
ACNE ☐   HEADACHE ☐   MOOD 😊 😐 ☹️
CRAMPS ☐   SORE BREASTS ☐   SLEEP 😊 😐 ☹️

· ·
· ·
· ·

Day 7 of Cycle

CRAVINGS ☐   BACKACHE ☐   ENERGY 😊 😐 ☹️
ACNE ☐   HEADACHE ☐   MOOD 😊 😐 ☹️
CRAMPS ☐   SORE BREASTS ☐   SLEEP 😊 😐 ☹️

· ·
· ·
· ·

J	F	M	A	M	J	J	A	S	O	N	D

1	2	3	4	5	6	7	8	9	10	11	12
13	14	15	16	17	18	19	20	21	22	23	24
25	26	27	28	29	30	31	*Cross off dates that do not apply this month				

KEY: ■ HEAVY ◢ MEDIUM ◩ LIGHT • SPOTTING ⊠ N/A

_____ DAYS SINCE LAST PERIOD ♥ EXPECT NEXT PERIOD AROUND _____

Day 1 of Cycle

CRAVINGS ☐   BACKACHE ☐   ENERGY ☺ 😐 ☹
ACNE ☐   HEADACHE ☐   MOOD ☺ 😐 ☹
CRAMPS ☐   SORE BREASTS ☐   SLEEP ☺ 😐 ☹

....
....
....

Day 2 of Cycle

CRAVINGS ☐   BACKACHE ☐   ENERGY ☺ 😐 ☹
ACNE ☐   HEADACHE ☐   MOOD ☺ 😐 ☹
CRAMPS ☐   SORE BREASTS ☐   SLEEP ☺ 😐 ☹

....
....
....

Day 3 of Cycle

CRAVINGS ☐   BACKACHE ☐   ENERGY ☺ 😐 ☹
ACNE ☐   HEADACHE ☐   MOOD ☺ 😐 ☹
CRAMPS ☐   SORE BREASTS ☐   SLEEP ☺ 😐 ☹

....
....
....

YEAR:_____

Day 4 of Cycle

CRAVINGS ☐   BACKACHE ☐   ENERGY 😀 😐 ☹️
ACNE ☐   HEADACHE ☐   MOOD 😀 😐 ☹️
CRAMPS ☐   SORE BREASTS ☐   SLEEP 😀 😐 ☹️

....
....
....

Day 5 of Cycle

CRAVINGS ☐   BACKACHE ☐   ENERGY 😀 😐 ☹️
ACNE ☐   HEADACHE ☐   MOOD 😀 😐 ☹️
CRAMPS ☐   SORE BREASTS ☐   SLEEP 😀 😐 ☹️

....
....
....

Day 6 of Cycle

CRAVINGS ☐   BACKACHE ☐   ENERGY 😀 😐 ☹️
ACNE ☐   HEADACHE ☐   MOOD 😀 😐 ☹️
CRAMPS ☐   SORE BREASTS ☐   SLEEP 😀 😐 ☹️

....
....
....

Day 7 of Cycle

CRAVINGS ☐   BACKACHE ☐   ENERGY 😀 😐 ☹️
ACNE ☐   HEADACHE ☐   MOOD 😀 😐 ☹️
CRAMPS ☐   SORE BREASTS ☐   SLEEP 😀 😐 ☹️

....
....
....

| J | F | M | A | M | J | J | A | S | O | N | D |

1	2	3	4	5	6	7	8	9	10	11	12
13	14	15	16	17	18	19	20	21	22	23	24
25	26	27	28	29	30	31	*Cross off dates that do not apply this month				

KEY: ■ HEAVY ◢ MEDIUM ◫ LIGHT • SPOTTING ⊠ N/A

_____ DAYS SINCE LAST PERIOD ♥ EXPECT NEXT PERIOD AROUND _____

Day 1 of Cycle

CRAVINGS ☐   BACKACHE ☐   ENERGY 😀 😐 🙁
ACNE ☐   HEADACHE ☐   MOOD 😀 😐 🙁
CRAMPS ☐   SORE BREASTS ☐   SLEEP 😀 😐 🙁

....
....
....

Day 2 of Cycle

CRAVINGS ☐   BACKACHE ☐   ENERGY 😀 😐 🙁
ACNE ☐   HEADACHE ☐   MOOD 😀 😐 🙁
CRAMPS ☐   SORE BREASTS ☐   SLEEP 😀 😐 🙁

....
....
....

Day 3 of Cycle

CRAVINGS ☐   BACKACHE ☐   ENERGY 😀 😐 🙁
ACNE ☐   HEADACHE ☐   MOOD 😀 😐 🙁
CRAMPS ☐   SORE BREASTS ☐   SLEEP 😀 😐 🙁

....
....
....

YEAR:_____

Day 4 of Cycle

CRAVINGS ☐   BACKACHE ☐   ENERGY 😊 😐 ☹
ACNE ☐   HEADACHE ☐   MOOD 😊 😐 ☹
CRAMPS ☐   SORE BREASTS ☐   SLEEP 😊 😐 ☹

....
....
....

Day 5 of Cycle

CRAVINGS ☐   BACKACHE ☐   ENERGY 😊 😐 ☹
ACNE ☐   HEADACHE ☐   MOOD 😊 😐 ☹
CRAMPS ☐   SORE BREASTS ☐   SLEEP 😊 😐 ☹

....
....
....

Day 6 of Cycle

CRAVINGS ☐   BACKACHE ☐   ENERGY 😊 😐 ☹
ACNE ☐   HEADACHE ☐   MOOD 😊 😐 ☹
CRAMPS ☐   SORE BREASTS ☐   SLEEP 😊 😐 ☹

....
....
....

Day 7 of Cycle

CRAVINGS ☐   BACKACHE ☐   ENERGY 😊 😐 ☹
ACNE ☐   HEADACHE ☐   MOOD 😊 😐 ☹
CRAMPS ☐   SORE BREASTS ☐   SLEEP 😊 😐 ☹

....
....
....

| J | F | M | A | M | J | J | A | S | O | N | D |

1	2	3	4	5	6	7	8	9	10	11	12
13	14	15	16	17	18	19	20	21	22	23	24
25	26	27	28	29	30	31	*Cross off dates that do not apply this month				

KEY: ■ HEAVY ◨ MEDIUM ▨ LIGHT • SPOTTING ⊠ N/A

_____ DAYS SINCE LAST PERIOD ♥ EXPECT NEXT PERIOD AROUND _____

Day 1 of Cycle

CRAVINGS ☐   BACKACHE ☐   ENERGY 🙂 😐 🙁
ACNE ☐   HEADACHE ☐   MOOD 🙂 😐 🙁
CRAMPS ☐   SORE BREASTS ☐   SLEEP 🙂 😐 🙁

....
....
....

Day 2 of Cycle

CRAVINGS ☐   BACKACHE ☐   ENERGY 🙂 😐 🙁
ACNE ☐   HEADACHE ☐   MOOD 🙂 😐 🙁
CRAMPS ☐   SORE BREASTS ☐   SLEEP 🙂 😐 🙁

....
....
....

Day 3 of Cycle

CRAVINGS ☐   BACKACHE ☐   ENERGY 🙂 😐 🙁
ACNE ☐   HEADACHE ☐   MOOD 🙂 😐 🙁
CRAMPS ☐   SORE BREASTS ☐   SLEEP 🙂 😐 🙁

....
....
....

Day 4 of Cycle

CRAVINGS ☐   BACKACHE ☐   ENERGY 😃 😐 😞
ACNE ☐   HEADACHE ☐   MOOD 😃 😐 😞
CRAMPS ☐   SORE BREASTS ☐   SLEEP 😃 😐 😞

....
....
....

Day 5 of Cycle

CRAVINGS ☐   BACKACHE ☐   ENERGY 😃 😐 😞
ACNE ☐   HEADACHE ☐   MOOD 😃 😐 😞
CRAMPS ☐   SORE BREASTS ☐   SLEEP 😃 😐 😞

....
....
....

Day 6 of Cycle

CRAVINGS ☐   BACKACHE ☐   ENERGY 😃 😐 😞
ACNE ☐   HEADACHE ☐   MOOD 😃 😐 😞
CRAMPS ☐   SORE BREASTS ☐   SLEEP 😃 😐 😞

....
....
....

Day 7 of Cycle

CRAVINGS ☐   BACKACHE ☐   ENERGY 😃 😐 😞
ACNE ☐   HEADACHE ☐   MOOD 😃 😐 😞
CRAMPS ☐   SORE BREASTS ☐   SLEEP 😃 😐 😞

....
....
....

| J | F | M | A | M | J | J | A | S | O | N | D |

1	2	3	4	5	6	7	8	9	10	11	12
13	14	15	16	17	18	19	20	21	22	23	24
25	26	27	28	29	30	31	*Cross off dates that do not apply this month				

KEY: ■ HEAVY ◤ MEDIUM ▨ LIGHT ● SPOTTING ⊠ N/A

_____ DAYS SINCE LAST PERIOD ♥ EXPECT NEXT PERIOD AROUND _____

Day 1 of Cycle

CRAVINGS ☐ BACKACHE ☐ ENERGY 😄 🙂 🙁
ACNE ☐ HEADACHE ☐ MOOD 😄 🙂 🙁
CRAMPS ☐ SORE BREASTS ☐ SLEEP 😄 🙂 🙁

....
....
....

Day 2 of Cycle

CRAVINGS ☐ BACKACHE ☐ ENERGY 😄 🙂 🙁
ACNE ☐ HEADACHE ☐ MOOD 😄 🙂 🙁
CRAMPS ☐ SORE BREASTS ☐ SLEEP 😄 🙂 🙁

....
....
....

Day 3 of Cycle

CRAVINGS ☐ BACKACHE ☐ ENERGY 😄 🙂 🙁
ACNE ☐ HEADACHE ☐ MOOD 😄 🙂 🙁
CRAMPS ☐ SORE BREASTS ☐ SLEEP 😄 🙂 🙁

....
....
....

YEAR:_____

Day 4 of Cycle

CRAVINGS ☐   BACKACHE ☐   ENERGY 🙂 😐 🙁
ACNE ☐   HEADACHE ☐   MOOD 🙂 😐 🙁
CRAMPS ☐   SORE BREASTS ☐   SLEEP 🙂 😐 🙁

....
....
....

Day 5 of Cycle

CRAVINGS ☐   BACKACHE ☐   ENERGY 🙂 😐 🙁
ACNE ☐   HEADACHE ☐   MOOD 🙂 😐 🙁
CRAMPS ☐   SORE BREASTS ☐   SLEEP 🙂 😐 🙁

....
....
....

Day 6 of Cycle

CRAVINGS ☐   BACKACHE ☐   ENERGY 🙂 😐 🙁
ACNE ☐   HEADACHE ☐   MOOD 🙂 😐 🙁
CRAMPS ☐   SORE BREASTS ☐   SLEEP 🙂 😐 🙁

....
....
....

Day 7 of Cycle

CRAVINGS ☐   BACKACHE ☐   ENERGY 🙂 😐 🙁
ACNE ☐   HEADACHE ☐   MOOD 🙂 😐 🙁
CRAMPS ☐   SORE BREASTS ☐   SLEEP 🙂 😐 🙁

....
....
....

1	2	3	4	5	6	7	8	9	10	11	12
13	14	15	16	17	18	19	20	21	22	23	24
25	26	27	28	29	30	31	*Cross off dates that do not apply this month				

KEY: ■ HEAVY ◤ MEDIUM ◩ LIGHT • SPOTTING ⊠ N/A

_____ DAYS SINCE LAST PERIOD 💜 EXPECT NEXT PERIOD AROUND _____

Day 1 of Cycle

CRAVINGS ☐   BACKACHE ☐   ENERGY 😀 😐 🙁
ACNE ☐   HEADACHE ☐   MOOD 😀 😐 🙁
CRAMPS ☐   SORE BREASTS ☐   SLEEP 😀 😐 🙁

....
....
....

Day 2 of Cycle

CRAVINGS ☐   BACKACHE ☐   ENERGY 😀 😐 🙁
ACNE ☐   HEADACHE ☐   MOOD 😀 😐 🙁
CRAMPS ☐   SORE BREASTS ☐   SLEEP 😀 😐 🙁

....
....
....

Day 3 of Cycle

CRAVINGS ☐   BACKACHE ☐   ENERGY 😀 😐 🙁
ACNE ☐   HEADACHE ☐   MOOD 😀 😐 🙁
CRAMPS ☐   SORE BREASTS ☐   SLEEP 😀 😐 🙁

....
....
....

Day 4 of Cycle

CRAVINGS ☐   BACKACHE ☐   ENERGY 😊 😐 😞
ACNE ☐   HEADACHE ☐   MOOD 😊 😐 😞
CRAMPS ☐   SORE BREASTS ☐   SLEEP 😊 😐 😞

....
....
....

Day 5 of Cycle

CRAVINGS ☐   BACKACHE ☐   ENERGY 😊 😐 😞
ACNE ☐   HEADACHE ☐   MOOD 😊 😐 😞
CRAMPS ☐   SORE BREASTS ☐   SLEEP 😊 😐 😞

....
....
....

Day 6 of Cycle

CRAVINGS ☐   BACKACHE ☐   ENERGY 😊 😐 😞
ACNE ☐   HEADACHE ☐   MOOD 😊 😐 😞
CRAMPS ☐   SORE BREASTS ☐   SLEEP 😊 😐 😞

....
....
....

Day 7 of Cycle

CRAVINGS ☐   BACKACHE ☐   ENERGY 😊 😐 😞
ACNE ☐   HEADACHE ☐   MOOD 😊 😐 😞
CRAMPS ☐   SORE BREASTS ☐   SLEEP 😊 😐 😞

....
....
....

1	2	3	4	5	6	7	8	9	10	11	12
13	14	15	16	17	18	19	20	21	22	23	24
25	26	27	28	29	30	31	*Cross off dates that do not apply this month				

KEY: ▨ HEAVY ◣ MEDIUM ▨ LIGHT • SPOTTING ⊠ N/A

_____ DAYS SINCE LAST PERIOD ♥ EXPECT NEXT PERIOD AROUND _____

Day 1 of Cycle

CRAVINGS ☐   BACKACHE ☐   ENERGY ☺ 😐 ☹
ACNE ☐   HEADACHE ☐   MOOD ☺ 😐 ☹
CRAMPS ☐   SORE BREASTS ☐   SLEEP ☺ 😐 ☹

....
....
....

Day 2 of Cycle

CRAVINGS ☐   BACKACHE ☐   ENERGY ☺ 😐 ☹
ACNE ☐   HEADACHE ☐   MOOD ☺ 😐 ☹
CRAMPS ☐   SORE BREASTS ☐   SLEEP ☺ 😐 ☹

....
....
....

Day 3 of Cycle

CRAVINGS ☐   BACKACHE ☐   ENERGY ☺ 😐 ☹
ACNE ☐   HEADACHE ☐   MOOD ☺ 😐 ☹
CRAMPS ☐   SORE BREASTS ☐   SLEEP ☺ 😐 ☹

....
....
....

YEAR:_____

Day 4 of Cycle

CRAVINGS ☐   BACKACHE ☐   ENERGY 😊 😐 ☹
ACNE ☐   HEADACHE ☐   MOOD 😊 😐 ☹
CRAMPS ☐   SORE BREASTS ☐   SLEEP 😊 😐 ☹

....
....
....

Day 5 of Cycle

CRAVINGS ☐   BACKACHE ☐   ENERGY 😊 😐 ☹
ACNE ☐   HEADACHE ☐   MOOD 😊 😐 ☹
CRAMPS ☐   SORE BREASTS ☐   SLEEP 😊 😐 ☹

....
....
....

Day 6 of Cycle

CRAVINGS ☐   BACKACHE ☐   ENERGY 😊 😐 ☹
ACNE ☐   HEADACHE ☐   MOOD 😊 😐 ☹
CRAMPS ☐   SORE BREASTS ☐   SLEEP 😊 😐 ☹

....
....
....

Day 7 of Cycle

CRAVINGS ☐   BACKACHE ☐   ENERGY 😊 😐 ☹
ACNE ☐   HEADACHE ☐   MOOD 😊 😐 ☹
CRAMPS ☐   SORE BREASTS ☐   SLEEP 😊 😐 ☹

....
....
....

J	F	m	A	m	J	J	A	S	O	N	D

1	2	3	4	5	6	7	8	9	10	11	12
13	14	15	16	17	18	19	20	21	22	23	24
25	26	27	28	29	30	31	*Cross off dates that do not apply this month				

KEY: ■ HEAVY ◩ MEDIUM ◨ LIGHT ⊡ SPOTTING ⊠ N/A

_____ DAYS SINCE LAST PERIOD ♥ EXPECT NEXT PERIOD AROUND _____

Day 1 of Cycle

CRAVINGS ☐   BACKACHE ☐   ENERGY ☺ 😐 ☹
ACNE ☐   HEADACHE ☐   MOOD ☺ 😐 ☹
CRAMPS ☐   SORE BREASTS ☐   SLEEP ☺ 😐 ☹

. . . .
. . . .
. . . .

Day 2 of Cycle

CRAVINGS ☐   BACKACHE ☐   ENERGY ☺ 😐 ☹
ACNE ☐   HEADACHE ☐   MOOD ☺ 😐 ☹
CRAMPS ☐   SORE BREASTS ☐   SLEEP ☺ 😐 ☹

. . . .
. . . .
. . . .

Day 3 of Cycle

CRAVINGS ☐   BACKACHE ☐   ENERGY ☺ 😐 ☹
ACNE ☐   HEADACHE ☐   MOOD ☺ 😐 ☹
CRAMPS ☐   SORE BREASTS ☐   SLEEP ☺ 😐 ☹

. . . .
. . . .
. . . .

Day 4 of Cycle

CRAVINGS ☐   BACKACHE ☐   ENERGY 😀 😐 🙁
ACNE ☐   HEADACHE ☐   MOOD 😀 😐 🙁
CRAMPS ☐   SORE BREASTS ☐   SLEEP 😀 😐 🙁

....
....
....

Day 5 of Cycle

CRAVINGS ☐   BACKACHE ☐   ENERGY 😀 😐 🙁
ACNE ☐   HEADACHE ☐   MOOD 😀 😐 🙁
CRAMPS ☐   SORE BREASTS ☐   SLEEP 😀 😐 🙁

....
....
....

Day 6 of Cycle

CRAVINGS ☐   BACKACHE ☐   ENERGY 😀 😐 🙁
ACNE ☐   HEADACHE ☐   MOOD 😀 😐 🙁
CRAMPS ☐   SORE BREASTS ☐   SLEEP 😀 😐 🙁

....
....
....

Day 7 of Cycle

CRAVINGS ☐   BACKACHE ☐   ENERGY 😀 😐 🙁
ACNE ☐   HEADACHE ☐   MOOD 😀 😐 🙁
CRAMPS ☐   SORE BREASTS ☐   SLEEP 😀 😐 🙁

....
....
....

1	2	3	4	5	6	7	8	9	10	11	12
13	14	15	16	17	18	19	20	21	22	23	24
25	26	27	28	29	30	31	*Cross off dates that do not apply this month				

KEY: ■ HEAVY ◩ MEDIUM ⬜ LIGHT ● SPOTTING ⊠ N/A

_____ DAYS SINCE LAST PERIOD ♥ EXPECT NEXT PERIOD AROUND _____

Day 1 of Cycle

CRAVINGS ☐   BACKACHE ☐   ENERGY 😊 😐 😞
ACNE ☐   HEADACHE ☐   MOOD 😊 😐 😞
CRAMPS ☐   SORE BREASTS ☐   SLEEP 😊 😐 😞

....
....
....

Day 2 of Cycle

CRAVINGS ☐   BACKACHE ☐   ENERGY 😊 😐 😞
ACNE ☐   HEADACHE ☐   MOOD 😊 😐 😞
CRAMPS ☐   SORE BREASTS ☐   SLEEP 😊 😐 😞

....
....
....

Day 3 of Cycle

CRAVINGS ☐   BACKACHE ☐   ENERGY 😊 😐 😞
ACNE ☐   HEADACHE ☐   MOOD 😊 😐 😞
CRAMPS ☐   SORE BREASTS ☐   SLEEP 😊 😐 😞

....
....
....

Day 4 of Cycle

CRAVINGS ☐   BACKACHE ☐   ENERGY 😃 😐 😞
ACNE ☐   HEADACHE ☐   MOOD 😃 😐 😞
CRAMPS ☐   SORE BREASTS ☐   SLEEP 😃 😐 😞

....
....
....

Day 5 of Cycle

CRAVINGS ☐   BACKACHE ☐   ENERGY 😃 😐 😞
ACNE ☐   HEADACHE ☐   MOOD 😃 😐 😞
CRAMPS ☐   SORE BREASTS ☐   SLEEP 😃 😐 😞

....
....
....

Day 6 of Cycle

CRAVINGS ☐   BACKACHE ☐   ENERGY 😃 😐 😞
ACNE ☐   HEADACHE ☐   MOOD 😃 😐 😞
CRAMPS ☐   SORE BREASTS ☐   SLEEP 😃 😐 😞

....
....
....

Day 7 of Cycle

CRAVINGS ☐   BACKACHE ☐   ENERGY 😃 😐 😞
ACNE ☐   HEADACHE ☐   MOOD 😃 😐 😞
CRAMPS ☐   SORE BREASTS ☐   SLEEP 😃 😐 😞

....
....
....

1	2	3	4	5	6	7	8	9	10	11	12
13	14	15	16	17	18	19	20	21	22	23	24
25	26	27	28	29	30	31	*Cross off dates that do not apply this month				

KEY: ■ HEAVY ◢ MEDIUM ◩ LIGHT • SPOTTING ⊠ N/A

_____ DAYS SINCE LAST PERIOD ♥ EXPECT NEXT PERIOD AROUND _____

Day 1 of Cycle

CRAVINGS ☐   BACKACHE ☐   ENERGY 😊 😐 🙁
ACNE ☐   HEADACHE ☐   MOOD 😊 😐 🙁
CRAMPS ☐   SORE BREASTS ☐   SLEEP 😊 😐 🙁

. . . .
. . . .
. . . .

Day 2 of Cycle

CRAVINGS ☐   BACKACHE ☐   ENERGY 😊 😐 🙁
ACNE ☐   HEADACHE ☐   MOOD 😊 😐 🙁
CRAMPS ☐   SORE BREASTS ☐   SLEEP 😊 😐 🙁

. . . .
. . . .
. . . .

Day 3 of Cycle

CRAVINGS ☐   BACKACHE ☐   ENERGY 😊 😐 🙁
ACNE ☐   HEADACHE ☐   MOOD 😊 😐 🙁
CRAMPS ☐   SORE BREASTS ☐   SLEEP 😊 😐 🙁

. . . .
. . . .
. . . .

Day 4 of Cycle

CRAVINGS ☐   BACKACHE ☐   ENERGY 😊 😐 ☹
ACNE ☐   HEADACHE ☐   MOOD 😊 😐 ☹
CRAMPS ☐   SORE BREASTS ☐   SLEEP 😊 😐 ☹

....
....
....

Day 5 of Cycle

CRAVINGS ☐   BACKACHE ☐   ENERGY 😊 😐 ☹
ACNE ☐   HEADACHE ☐   MOOD 😊 😐 ☹
CRAMPS ☐   SORE BREASTS ☐   SLEEP 😊 😐 ☹

....
....
....

Day 6 of Cycle

CRAVINGS ☐   BACKACHE ☐   ENERGY 😊 😐 ☹
ACNE ☐   HEADACHE ☐   MOOD 😊 😐 ☹
CRAMPS ☐   SORE BREASTS ☐   SLEEP 😊 😐 ☹

....
....
....

Day 7 of Cycle

CRAVINGS ☐   BACKACHE ☐   ENERGY 😊 😐 ☹
ACNE ☐   HEADACHE ☐   MOOD 😊 😐 ☹
CRAMPS ☐   SORE BREASTS ☐   SLEEP 😊 😐 ☹

....
....
....

(J)	(F)	(M)	(A)	(M)	(J)	(J)	(A)	(S)	(O)	(N)	(D)

1	2	3	4	5	6	7	8	9	10	11	12
13	14	15	16	17	18	19	20	21	22	23	24
25	26	27	28	29	30	31	*Cross off dates that do not apply this month				

KEY: ▮ HEAVY ◣ MEDIUM ◩ LIGHT • SPOTTING ⊠ N/A

_____ DAYS SINCE LAST PERIOD ♥ EXPECT NEXT PERIOD AROUND _____

Day 1 of Cycle

CRAVINGS ☐   BACKACHE ☐   ENERGY 😊 😐 😟
ACNE ☐   HEADACHE ☐   MOOD 😊 😐 😟
CRAMPS ☐   SORE BREASTS ☐   SLEEP 😊 😐 😟

....
....
....

Day 2 of Cycle

CRAVINGS ☐   BACKACHE ☐   ENERGY 😊 😐 😟
ACNE ☐   HEADACHE ☐   MOOD 😊 😐 😟
CRAMPS ☐   SORE BREASTS ☐   SLEEP 😊 😐 😟

....
....
....

Day 3 of Cycle

CRAVINGS ☐   BACKACHE ☐   ENERGY 😊 😐 😟
ACNE ☐   HEADACHE ☐   MOOD 😊 😐 😟
CRAMPS ☐   SORE BREASTS ☐   SLEEP 😊 😐 😟

....
....
....

Day 4 of Cycle

CRAVINGS ☐   BACKACHE ☐   ENERGY 😀 😐 ☹️
ACNE ☐   HEADACHE ☐   MOOD 😀 😐 ☹️
CRAMPS ☐   SORE BREASTS ☐   SLEEP 😀 😐 ☹️

....
....
....

Day 5 of Cycle

CRAVINGS ☐   BACKACHE ☐   ENERGY 😀 😐 ☹️
ACNE ☐   HEADACHE ☐   MOOD 😀 😐 ☹️
CRAMPS ☐   SORE BREASTS ☐   SLEEP 😀 😐 ☹️

....
....
....

Day 6 of Cycle

CRAVINGS ☐   BACKACHE ☐   ENERGY 😀 😐 ☹️
ACNE ☐   HEADACHE ☐   MOOD 😀 😐 ☹️
CRAMPS ☐   SORE BREASTS ☐   SLEEP 😀 😐 ☹️

....
....
....

Day 7 of Cycle

CRAVINGS ☐   BACKACHE ☐   ENERGY 😀 😐 ☹️
ACNE ☐   HEADACHE ☐   MOOD 😀 😐 ☹️
CRAMPS ☐   SORE BREASTS ☐   SLEEP 😀 😐 ☹️

....
....
....

| J | F | m | A | m | J | J | A | S | O | N | D |

1	2	3	4	5	6	7	8	9	10	11	12
13	14	15	16	17	18	19	20	21	22	23	24
25	26	27	28	29	30	31	*Cross off dates that do not apply this month				

KEY: ▮ HEAVY ◣ MEDIUM ▨ LIGHT ⊡ SPOTTING ⊠ N/A

_____ DAYS SINCE LAST PERIOD ♥ EXPECT NEXT PERIOD AROUND _____

Day 1 of Cycle

CRAVINGS ☐   BACKACHE ☐   ENERGY 😊 😐 ☹
ACNE ☐   HEADACHE ☐   MOOD 😊 😐 ☹
CRAMPS ☐   SORE BREASTS ☐   SLEEP 😊 😐 ☹

....
....
....

Day 2 of Cycle

CRAVINGS ☐   BACKACHE ☐   ENERGY 😊 😐 ☹
ACNE ☐   HEADACHE ☐   MOOD 😊 😐 ☹
CRAMPS ☐   SORE BREASTS ☐   SLEEP 😊 😐 ☹

....
....
....

Day 3 of Cycle

CRAVINGS ☐   BACKACHE ☐   ENERGY 😊 😐 ☹
ACNE ☐   HEADACHE ☐   MOOD 😊 😐 ☹
CRAMPS ☐   SORE BREASTS ☐   SLEEP 😊 😐 ☹

....
....
....

Day 4 of Cycle

CRAVINGS ☐   BACKACHE ☐   ENERGY 😊 😐 ☹️
ACNE ☐   HEADACHE ☐   MOOD 😊 😐 ☹️
CRAMPS ☐   SORE BREASTS ☐   SLEEP 😊 😐 ☹️

....
....
....

Day 5 of Cycle

CRAVINGS ☐   BACKACHE ☐   ENERGY 😊 😐 ☹️
ACNE ☐   HEADACHE ☐   MOOD 😊 😐 ☹️
CRAMPS ☐   SORE BREASTS ☐   SLEEP 😊 😐 ☹️

....
....
....

Day 6 of Cycle

CRAVINGS ☐   BACKACHE ☐   ENERGY 😊 😐 ☹️
ACNE ☐   HEADACHE ☐   MOOD 😊 😐 ☹️
CRAMPS ☐   SORE BREASTS ☐   SLEEP 😊 😐 ☹️

....
....
....

Day 7 of Cycle

CRAVINGS ☐   BACKACHE ☐   ENERGY 😊 😐 ☹️
ACNE ☐   HEADACHE ☐   MOOD 😊 😐 ☹️
CRAMPS ☐   SORE BREASTS ☐   SLEEP 😊 😐 ☹️

....
....
....

J	F	M	A	M	J	J	A	S	O	N	D

1	2	3	4	5	6	7	8	9	10	11	12
13	14	15	16	17	18	19	20	21	22	23	24
25	26	27	28	29	30	31	*Cross off dates that do not apply this month				

KEY: �rect HEAVY ◢ MEDIUM ◳ LIGHT • SPOTING ⊠ N/A

_____ DAYS SINCE LAST PERIOD 💜 EXPECT NEXT PERIOD AROUND _____

Day 1 of Cycle

CRAVINGS ☐   BACKACHE ☐   ENERGY 😊 😐 😞
ACNE ☐   HEADACHE ☐   MOOD 😊 😐 😞
CRAMPS ☐   SORE BREASTS ☐   SLEEP 😊 😐 😞

....
....
....

Day 2 of Cycle

CRAVINGS ☐   BACKACHE ☐   ENERGY 😊 😐 😞
ACNE ☐   HEADACHE ☐   MOOD 😊 😐 😞
CRAMPS ☐   SORE BREASTS ☐   SLEEP 😊 😐 😞

....
....
....

Day 3 of Cycle

CRAVINGS ☐   BACKACHE ☐   ENERGY 😊 😐 😞
ACNE ☐   HEADACHE ☐   MOOD 😊 😐 😞
CRAMPS ☐   SORE BREASTS ☐   SLEEP 😊 😐 😞

....
....
....

Day 4 of Cycle

CRAVINGS ☐   BACKACHE ☐   ENERGY 😊 😐 ☹
ACNE ☐   HEADACHE ☐   MOOD 😊 😐 ☹
CRAMPS ☐   SORE BREASTS ☐   SLEEP 😊 😐 ☹

....
....
....

Day 5 of Cycle

CRAVINGS ☐   BACKACHE ☐   ENERGY 😊 😐 ☹
ACNE ☐   HEADACHE ☐   MOOD 😊 😐 ☹
CRAMPS ☐   SORE BREASTS ☐   SLEEP 😊 😐 ☹

....
....
....

Day 6 of Cycle

CRAVINGS ☐   BACKACHE ☐   ENERGY 😊 😐 ☹
ACNE ☐   HEADACHE ☐   MOOD 😊 😐 ☹
CRAMPS ☐   SORE BREASTS ☐   SLEEP 😊 😐 ☹

....
....
....

Day 7 of Cycle

CRAVINGS ☐   BACKACHE ☐   ENERGY 😊 😐 ☹
ACNE ☐   HEADACHE ☐   MOOD 😊 😐 ☹
CRAMPS ☐   SORE BREASTS ☐   SLEEP 😊 😐 ☹

....
....
....

Made in the USA
Monee, IL
13 July 2023